GLENDALOUGH

Michael Rodgers & Marcus Losack

Glendalough
A Celtic Pilgrimage

the columba press

First published, 1996, by
the columba press
55A Spruce Avenue, Stillorgan Industrial Park,
Blackrock, Co Dublin
Second Printing 1996
Third Printing 1998
Fourth Printing 1999
Fifth Printing 2001

Cover by Bill Bolger
Illustrations by Natalie Connolly*
Origination by The Columba Press
Printed in Ireland by Colour Books Ltd, Dublin

ISBN 1 85607 173 1

Acknowledgements
The authors and the publishers are grateful to the following for permission to use material which is in their copyright: Seamus Heaney and Faber and Faber Ltd for *St Kevin and the Blackbird*; HarperCollins Publishers for a quotation from *A World Made Whole* by Esther de Waal; Darton, Longman and Todd for a quotation from *The Celtic Vision* by Esther de Waal; Noel Dermot O'Donoghue and T & T Clark Ltd for quotations from *Introduction to Celtic Christianity* edited by James Mackey; Colin Smythe Ltd for a quotation from *Treasury of Irish Saints* by John Irvine; The Gallery Press for a quotation from *Sing Me Creation* by Desmond O'Grady; David Higham Associates for *The Eternal Cross* by Elizabeth Jennings, from *Times and Seasons* (Carcanet Press); Harper San Francisco for various quotations from *Earth Prayers* edited by Roberts and Amedon; Desmond Forristal for his translation on page 117 and for a quotation from his *The Man in the Middle*; Imogen Stuart for the use of her woodcarving on page 100; Edward C Sellner for quotations from his *Wisdom of the Celtic Saints* (Ave Maria) and his article on 'Soulfriendship' in *Cistercian Studies Quarterly*; Reed Consumer Books for the quotation from *The Little Prince* by Antoin de Saint Exupery (Heinemann); SPCK and David Adam for his prayer *Circle Me, Lord* from his book *The Edge of Glory*. Psalm quotations are from the New Revised Standard Version Bible: copyright © 1993 and 1989 by the Division of Christian Education of the National Council of the Churches of Christ in the USA. Used by permission. All rights reserved.
If we have failed to trace any copyright material, we offer our apologies and invite the copyright holders to contact the publishers.

* Illustrations on pages 32, 55, 56, 109, 116 and 122 are from old printed sources.

Contents

Preface

Michael Rodgers and Marcus Losack first met in Glendalough three years ago. Michael arrived in Glendalough in 1992, after spending twenty years in Kenya and six years on the General Council of St Patrick's Missionary Society, Kiltegan, Co Wicklow. He came to explore the spirit of Glendalough but this quickly developed into sharing his insights with other people who came to visit the valley. He works with individuals and groups, introducing people to Glendalough's history by a prayerful journey through the valley.

Marcus had arrived back in Ireland from the Holy Land, where he had been teaching at St George's College in Jerusalem, and leading pilgrimages to the ancient desert monasteries of Egypt and Sinai. He is Director of Céile Dé, an ecumenical organisation in Ireland specialising in the development of study-pilgrimage programmes in Celtic spirituality, and lives at Annamoe, near Glendalough in Co Wicklow, with his wife, Noeleen, and children, Seán, Aidan and Gemma.

'We were drawn, like many others before us, by the beauty and fascination of this place. We had both moved to a new situation in our lives, after several years of service in different churches. We came together from two different denominations and cultures, but shared the same basic faith and spiritual traditions. After two years working together writing this book, we see little sense in maintaining the divisions which fracture the visible unity of the churches. We have discovered that what we can achieve together is far more than we could achieve alone. We hope this book will contribute towards a spirit of ecumenism

and encourage the churches to explore new ways of working
together towards unity, so that we may find peace and reconcil-
iation together, in honour of God.

'We would like to express our very sincere thanks to those who
have helped us with this book. To Natalie Connolly, whose
drawings have greatly enhanced the text. To Gill McCarthy who
acted as midwife and editor, breathing a spirit of life into our
work at a difficult moment. Without her help this book might
never have seen the light of day. We are indebted to some recent
pilgrims to Glendalough who left their poems and reflections
behind them. We are also deeply grateful to Esther de Waal and
Ed Sellner, whose writings on the Celtic tradition continue to inspire us. We especially thank Esther de Waal for writing the
foreword for this book.'

Foreword

Esther de Waal

More and more people are recognising their need to make a pilgrimage, and Glendalough draws people to itself today as it has always done throughout history. For it is as true now as it was then that a holy place carries power. To be on pilgrimage is to move into a world where the dividing line between past and present, between this world and the next, between what we call sacred and what we call secular, dissolves. The outward journey is also a journey inwards. We have to be prepared to let go of the accustomed patterns and controls that we impose on our daily lives, and instead be ready to be open to what lies beyond – and what is most often expressed in symbol, image, poetry.

For this opening up to happen, we need guides and guidance. This is what this book does so admirably. Here are two friends (and the Celtic tradition knew so much about the God-given gift of friendship) for whom the past is a living experience that they want to share with others. They also know, as the Celtic peoples knew, that for any fullness of life there must be a holding together of the light and the shadow, and the reality of that is movingly shown as the pilgrimage develops. To encounter Glendalough in this way is to learn a little more about God, about one's own self, about the saints and the angels, about the earth itself. This book offers the opportunity to become, however briefly, one of those Celtic *peregrini* (pilgrims, wanderers, seekers, exiles, the word carries connotations of all of these), in search of the place of their resurrection, which is the deepest and truest self in Christ. Here is something which is timeless, part of our earliest past as it is part of the modern world, and I am only too happy to say God speed to all those who set out to uncover the riches that this holy place can bring.

Glossary

Glendalough:	*der:* Gleann dá locha – Valley of Two Lakes
Cillín:	A small church. *pron* Killeen
Caoimhín:	Kevin. *pron* Queeveen
Coemgen:	Old Irish form of Kevin. *pron* Cave-yin
Coemlug:	Kevin's father. *pron* Cave-lug
Coemella:	Kevin's mother. *pron* Cave-ella
Daimhliag:	An old Irish stone church. *pron* Davliag
Pattern:	Festival of Patron Saint (June 3rd).
Cloigtheach:	Bell house. *pron* Clug-hagh
Nave:	Main body of a church, outside the sanctuary
Chancel:	Area of a church where altar is situated
Teampall :	Church. *pron* champall
Muire:	Máire or Mary. *pron* Mwir-eh
Díseart:	Desert or hermitage. *pron* deeshurt
Caher:	Homestead. *pron* Caher
Loch:	Lake
Peist:	Large reptile or monster. *pron* pesht
Anamchara :	Soul-friend. *pron* anum-khara

From Hollywood to Glendalough

Who saw everything
to the ends of the land,
began at the start
of a primary road.

Who saw the mysteries
knew secret things
went on a long journey
found the whole story
cut in stone.

(Desmond O'Grady, *Sing Me Creation*)

In west Wicklow, at the foot of the mountains, there is a little place called Hollywood. In Irish, it is called *Cillín Chaoimhín* or the little church of Kevin. It has its own St Kevin's Bed, St Kevin's Cave, St Kevin's Chair and St Kevin's Well. From Hollywood an ancient roadway through the Wicklow Gap, marked by crosses and stones, guided the way of pilgrims over the mountains to the holy ground of Glendalough. This old road was known as St Kevin's Road.

We do not know which road Kevin may have taken when he first came to Glendalough. *The Metrical Life of St Kevin*, in Irish, simply tells us that he, 'crossed the summits with an angel and built a monastery among the Glens'.[1] This is reflected in a local tradition that Kevin came to Glendalough for the first time over the mountains. After his death it is likely that the old road through the Wicklow Gap became a pilgrim road, when Glendalough became famous as a pilgrimage centre in the sixth and seventh centuries. Pilgrims came to Glendalough in their thousands with a popular belief that, 'for obtaining remission of their sins from God, it is the same for anyone to visit Rome, and to visit the relics and beds of Coemgen'.[2]

The old St Kevin's Road is marked by crosses and stones and early Christian church sites at Dunboyke and Templeteenawn. Near Templeteenawn Church there is a stone known as the Piper's Rock, 'where people going to the Pattern at the churches used to stop; they used to have tents there and music and dancing'.[3]

A few miles away, on top of a hill at Togher, there is an old seventh-century cross, cut in a granite boulder known as 'The Wooden Cross'. There is another cross on a granite pillar a few miles further on at Granabeg.

The Granabeg Cross

The best known stone from the old pilgrim road was located near Hollywood. It is a labyrinth stone which was known locally as 'The Walls of Troy'. It is now in the National Museum in

Dublin. Price remarks, '... as well as typifying the difficulties and dangers of the Christian life, the labyrinth stone marked a spot where the pilgrim entered a toilsome journey through the desolate mountainous country, where prayer and religious fervour would be needed to help him on his way'.[4]

At the top of the Wicklow Gap it is possible to stand on a remnant of the old St Kevin's Road. It is about ten feet wide and made up of large rough granite stones, laid down across the bog. There is a wonderful view in all directions, westwards towards the great plains of Ireland and eastwards towards the sea, shining and glistening on the horizon on a sunny day. We can imagine pilgrims standing there long ago, looking back along the rough way they had travelled and giving thanks to God for bringing them safely to this point in their journey. We can imagine also the sense of expectancy and excitement as they looked down the valley to the east, knowing that the end of the road was almost in sight. Already, part of the purpose of their pilgrimage had been realised in telling their story and sharing their problems with those who accompanied them on the way.

At the crossroads, where the Wicklow Gap road meets the Laragh to Glendalough road, another old stone can be found with two crosses on it. Pilgrims would have gathered here for a prayer before entering Glendalough, no doubt feeling relief after making the hazardous journey and looking forward to completing their pilgrimage in the holy places of the valley.

The crossroads is a good place to stop and focus attention on the purpose of our own journey. Scripture reminds us to 'stand beside the earliest roads, ask the pathways of old which is the way to good, and walk it; thus you will find rest for your souls' (Jer 6:16). Every pilgrim came to Glendalough for a purpose. What is your purpose? What are you looking for? What do you want?

The cross at the crossroads

And did you get what
you wanted from this life, even so?
I did.
And what did you want?
To call myself beloved, to feel myself
Beloved on the earth.

(Raymond Carver, *Late Fragment*)

Here, we may like to ask permission, with respect, to enter this ancient and holy place of pilgrimage, opening ourselves to its mystery and magic. Glendalough is ready to reveal its wonder, if we are willing to spend time moving slowly through the valley.

We offer you this little book to be your guide. We have walked these roads many, many times and tried to enter into the spirit of the place in the company of the spirits of ages past. We have been privileged to walk in the present time with many people from different parts of the world, listening to their stories as they have shared ours. We have gained great insights from their experience and they have contributed valuable material to this guidebook.

We hope that you will know yourself as a pilgrim in Glendalough, and find peace in this beautiful natural environment. Glendalough expresses its beauty and holiness through many different moods; sometimes sombre, sometimes sunny, always haunting and mysterious. May God bless you! May the spirits of St Kevin and St Laurence and all the pilgrim people of Glendalough accompany you on your journey through this enchanted valley.

The Labyrinth Stone

The Story and Legends of St Kevin

A soldier of Christ into the land of Ireland
A high name over land and sea
Coemgen, the holy fair warrior
In the valley of the two broad lakes'
(*Feilire of Oengus* c. 800)

The most beautiful experience we can have
is the mysterious. (*Einstein*)

We will be telling parts of Kevin's story elsewhere in this book, as we travel through the valley on our pilgrim way. There are many, many stories handed down to us; just a few examples are given here to complete a picture of this remarkable person. It is important to remember that the stories about St Kevin's life were handed on firstly by oral tradition, only to be written down five hundred years after his death, so should not be taken too historically or interpreted in a literal way. At the same time, they may well hold nuggets of historical information which can provide insights into his life and experience. Stories, myths and legends survive primarily because they express deeper truths that the heart understands. It is in this spirit we explore some of the stories and legends here, and try to understand what meaning St Kevin may still hold for us today.

Kevin was at heart a hermit and a Christian mystic. He was a determined ascetic whose great strength and endurance sprang from his extraordinary faith and commitment to monastic celibacy and the teachings of the Desert Spiritual Tradition. As well as being a hermit and founder of monasteries, he wrote poetry and prose, including a Rule for monks in Irish verse. We will see he was also a gentle, loving and kind person, with an extraordinary and unusual affinity to nature, especially the animals and birds. He was someone deeply attracted to the poetic experience of the hermit life; courageous in his desire to draw out to the edge to test his strength and endurance. He chose hardship quite deliberately; his cell was on the dark side of the lake which remained in shadow for six months of the year. Why was this so? Perhaps it was a desire to feel very exposed; to test himself to the limit, and through that test find his own deepest strength, but perhaps most of all it was through an ascetic way of life that he found the poetry of his own soul.

The sources for Kevin's story are found in six books. Three of these are in Latin and three in Irish. The earliest source of the Latin Lives is in the *Codex Kilkenniensis* in Marsh's Library in Dublin. This was probably written in the eleventh century, five to six hundred years after Kevin's death. The Irish Lives were transcribed by Michael O'Clery in 1629, from the old books that relied heavily on oral traditions and pilgrim's tales.[1]

The year of Kevin's birth is generally given as 498 CE but there are good reasons to doubt this. The Annals of Ulster record the date of his death as 618 CE. If correct this means he would have lived one hundred and twenty years – very unlikely in the cold and damp conditions which prevail in Glendalough. It is more likely that he was born somewhere in the middle of the sixth century.

St Kevin came from a royal line of the tribe of Dal-Mesincorb. His father was named Coemlug and his mother was called Coemella. Even before he was born there was promise of great things to come. An angel appeared to Coemella and informed her that she was to have a boy and should call him Coemgen, who would be 'dear to both God and man ... and the father over many monks'. When Kevin was being brought to the priest Cronan, for baptism, legend says that 'a person appeared and breathed on the child, blessing him and calling him Coemgen'.

Cronan believed this was an angel and said, 'So he shall always be called Coemgen (which means the fair-begotten or beautiful born) for he will be most beautiful!'[2] Cronan saw his bright future and committed himself and all he had to St Kevin's service as his first monk. The lives of the saints always began with miraculous events such as these.

Like so many of the Celtic saints, Kevin had a close relationship with nature and a great love of animals. From a very early age he gained a reputation for doing extraordinary things. One story describes how, when he was a child, a white cow came to his parents' house every morning and evening with milk for him. We are left wondering what meaning or significance was attached to these original stories. In Irish mythology, the cow was considered sacred. An old Irish proverb says, 'the cow is one of the pleasant trees of paradise'. There was an otherworld, mystical significance attached especially to the white cow, which was associated with brightness and wisdom. In Irish folk tradition, milk was regarded as one of the sources of poetry. Perhaps animal stories were used to explain the qualities of Kevin's character, and especially the gifts of wisdom, poetry and brightness associated with his name.

Kevin gained an early reputation for performing miracles. His parents knew that he was an extraordinarily gifted and unusual child and at the early age of twelve they sent him to three holy men, Eogan, Lochan and Enna, for religious instruction and spiritual formation. Their monastery was probably at Kilnamanagh in Tallaght, County Dublin, although there is another opinion that it was at Glenealy, in County Wicklow.

Kevin seems to have been propelled into religious life by his parents, perhaps following the prophecies at the time of his birth. However, he had his own dream to follow and, leaving the monastery at an early age, he ran away and hid in the Wicklow Mountains. Eventually, he came to Glendalough for the first time and made his way to the Upper Lake, to a place he thought was ideal for solitude and prayer. He lived a very simple and austere life in the hollow of a tree, eating only herbs and drinking water. Legend tells us that he stayed there for many days, undisturbed by anyone, until one day a cow which had been brought to graze in the area came to him and began to lick his garments. She continued to do this every day until her owner began to be suspicious that something unusual was happening when she began to produce great quantities of milk. The owner asked his herdsmen to watch the cow closely, which led to the discovery of Kevin's retreat. Word of its location reached his three teachers, Eogan, Lochan and Enna who came and took him back to the monastery.

What was the dream and spirit inside St Kevin, that drew him to Glendalough? He was born into a time and a land that was alive with conversion to Christianity. Holy wells and places such as Loch Derg and Croagh Patrick were already vibrant places of pilgrimage for Christians. We can imagine the excitement and debate amongst the young in such an environment. Kevin also came from a privileged background, and may well have discovered the Bronze Age tomb on the side of the cliff at Glendalough during a hunting expedition over the mountains, taken with other young nobles.

The virtues of celibacy and virginity were new Christian values, introduced into Ireland by St Patrick. In pre-Christian Ireland, as with other nature religions, fertility was not only valued, it was considered sacred and vital for survival. There is plenty of evidence that this was true of the Celts. The presence of 'Sheela na Gig' images in many old churches would indicate that human sexuality was certainly not offensive. Yet the call to the celibate and ascetic life attracted many, and somewhere in the depths of his being, this vigorous, handsome and healthy son of a chieftain felt the call to deny himself, take up his cross and follow in the footsteps of Jesus. That call led him to the dark and sombre side of the valley at Glendalough.

After his return to the monastery at Kilnamanagh, Kevin continued to work miracles which greatly impressed those around him. He continued his studies, eventually going to stay with Bishop Lugid who ordained him to the ministry of the priesthood. Lugid directed him with some friends to found a new monastery at Cluainduach. The location of this monastery is unknown, but it is said that he collected there many companions for Christ. It is apparent that he must have been a charismatic and effective leader, even though we are told he spent most of his time in his cell, praying and continuing to work miracles. His heart was restless, however, and after establishing this monastery, accompanied by some monks he set out towards the place where he had found solitude when he was young. The lure of Glendalough had obviously never left him. He once again began to follow the dream of his own calling and inspired others to join him.

Whilst Kevin's life was driven by the desire for solitude and asceticism, his story does not evade some disturbing moments which he experienced in his personal and spiritual development. Stories of Kevin's gentlessness and kindness to animals have to be reconciled with other more painful accounts of his struggle with celibacy and conflicts he experienced, especially in his relationships with women.

One story, linked to the time of his training in the monastery at Kilnamanagh, for example, describes how a young girl saw him in the fields with his brethren and fell passionately in love with him. She pursued him in many ways, but Kevin resisted all her advances. One day she came upon him alone, embraced him fondly and asked him tenderly to lie with her. At this Kevin rushed away, and finding a bed of stinging nettles he stripped off his clothes and rolled in them naked. The girl still pursued him, and quickly dressing, he took a bunch of nettles and began to beat her with them around her face, hands and feet. She quickly realised the hopelessness of her pursuit and fell on her knees, begging forgiveness from Kevin and from God. She also promised that she would dedicate her life to God, and became a nun.[3]

The story emphasises Kevin's extreme religious fervour and also his struggle to remain celibate. Kevin's commitment to celibacy is pictured against the natural instincts and passions of a young couple mutually attracted and longing to express their love and affection. It is also a very sad story; the poignant tale of the pushing away of human love for something perceived as greater. Perhaps it illustrates the struggles of celibacy, appreciating the sacredness and wonder of the gift of love and human sexuality, but even this is put aside to serve God. We can appreciate the depth and beauty of the story with all its passion and longing, whilst recoiling from its violence. It shows that at the heart of Kevin's experience and his quest for holiness there was real struggle.

A popular version of this story, which probably evolved out of the original story given above, describes an incident which is said to have taken place in Glendalough, and names the woman as Kathleen. It continues the theme of seduction but presents Kathleen even more strongly as temptress. She attempts to seduce Kevin in his cave and he expels her, pushing her into the lake where she drowns. This story may have been used by guides in the nineteenth century to entertain visitors but it is unhistorical and offensive to many.

There is another story concerning a woman who entered St Kevin's life; he was an old man by this time. She may have been a sister from St Mary's Church; her name was Cassayr. The story tells of St Kevin praying for the soul of a murdered person. While he prayed, he levitated, which is how Cassayr found him. She was shocked by his appearance and ragged clothing and begged him to receive better garments from her. He rejected this offer, through fear of temptation, which saddened Cassayr. However, she still placed herself and all her religious congregation under his Rule. Legend says that an angel of the Lord removed his old, rough garments and clothed him in the garments offered by Cassayr.[4] Perhaps this story hints that Kevin's attitude towards women softened as he aged, and he was able to accept a spontaneous and generous gesture of love and concern without feeling compromised.

As a young man, Kevin gained a great reputation for performing miracles. Another story describes how, one day, he went
into the woods with an older monk also called Coemgen. The
younger Coemgen was supposed to bring fire but forgot it completely. The older Coemgen said, 'Brother, run quickly for the
fire and bring it with you'. St. Kevin asked how he would carry
it and was told, somewhat angrily by his teacher, 'In your
bosom!' Kevin then went and collected the fire, but miraculously
neither his flesh nor his clothes were burned. The teacher immediately said, 'O holy youth, I see that you are full of the Holy
Ghost and that thou oughtest to rule over our community'.[5]

These stories can hold different levels of meaning for us today.
We can imagine the young trainee-hermit going into the woods
for guidance and instruction. Perhaps his teacher was an older
hermit, guiding Kevin in the path of contemplation and prayer.
The story is intriguing. Was the old monk really talking about
fire in the literal sense, strengthening the young monks growing
reputation for miracles? Was Kevin so motivated, he simply did
not feel the pain of burning fire? Like all good stories, we are left
pondering the meaning and mystery of the story which has endured through the ages. If we remember these tales were handed
on for hundreds of years by oral tradition we can see how many
different threads may have become woven through them and
how misunderstandings and misinterpretations may have arisen.

We are told that Kevin did not like the fame which his miracles
brought him and decided to leave the monastery and go away to
a remote place where he could be alone to practise a more austere and contemplative lifestyle. Thus the pattern of his life
emerges; times of community and responsibility for others;
times of solitude and isolation. The writer of the Latin Life men-
tions that in the lower valley, where two clear rivers flow together,
St Kevin founded a great monastery. Many flocked to him from
the surrounding countryside and became monks in this place. It
is said that many other cells and monasteries were founded
from Glendalough in the Province of Leinster. For Kevin, how-

ever, when the monastery was established, he once again heard the call of the hermitage.

He left others in charge and set out alone to the upper part of the valley about a mile distant, where he built a small cell for himself in a narrow place between the mountain and the lake. It is generally accepted that this is the place known today as Templenaskellig. He ordered his monks to send him no food and not to approach him except on urgent business. He lived there in complete solitude for at least four years, praying and fasting without a fire or roof over his head. It was not known how he survived but his diet would probably have included plants and berries from the forest, herbs and nuts and perhaps even some fish, with a constant supply of heavenly food.

The experience of prayer and austerity, instead of hardening Kevin, enabled him to express his gentleness and become more at one with himself, with creation and with God. He lived in a place beneath the cliffs on the shores of the Upper Lake, which remains in shadow for at least six months of the year. The reality of this must be woven through our understanding of Kevin's life at this time. It is also a very beautiful place, where even today there is a great atmosphere of peace and seclusion. It was here that Kevin's desire for solitude was realised, and he developed close relationships with even the wildest animals. It is said, for example, that the wild beasts from the woods and the mountains came and tamely drank water from his hands:

> Where Kevin was the eagle came
> Down from the highest mountain tame,
> And sat amongst the lesser birds
> To hear the wisdom of his words.

> The speckled trout would swiftly glide
> To the reedy water's side,
> And there the mountain deer would stand
> To eat the green moss from his hand.

The snarling wolf and savage boar
Lay down together at his door
And so defied all natural laws
About the cave where Kevin was.[6]

St Kevin's Bed

Another story involved a huntsman and a wild boar. A huntsman entered the valley on a certain day, following his dogs
which were engaged in the pursuit of a wild boar. The boar ran
into St Kevin's oratory but the dogs, not daring to follow, lay
down before the door. St Kevin remained praying beneath a
tree, while many birds were seen perched upon his head and
shoulders. They flew around him and 'warbled sweet hymns in
honour of God's servant'. Surprised at what he saw, the hunter
called away his dogs. He left the boar at liberty there because of
the reverence he felt towards the holy anchorite.[7]

Kevin is also said to have prayed for one hour every night in the
cold waters of the lake where a monster used to try to distract
and annoy him by curling itself around his body, biting and
stinging him. In another story he banished a monster from the
Lower Lake to the Upper Lake. As Kevin lived alone at the
Upper Lake, in effect, he took the monster to himself. It was said
that the fervour of his prayer, his patience and the fire of God's
love in him, rendered the monster harmless. The imagery used
is so erotic and intimate, however, that it leaves us wondering
what and who the monster was that Kevin experienced in his
life, at first so painfully?

Kevin's story also suggests that, well into old age, he was still as-
sailed by doubts, fears, and various longings which made his
heart restless. On one occasion, for example, Kevin was thinking
of making a pilgrimage. Another hermit called Garbhan became
aware of this and suggested that it was better for Kevin to remain
in one spot, serving the Lord, than to go about from place to
place in his old age, saying that 'no bird on the wing can hatch its
eggs'. Accepting this advice, Kevin decided not to make the pilgrimage.[8] After a time of prayer and fasting, legend also says,
that Kevin was nearly persuaded by satan, who appeared to him
in the bright form of an angel, to quit the valley and travel
abroad. St Munna of Taghmon discovered in a vision that this
was a deception, and sent messengers to Glendalough with a
word of warning. As a result, Kevin decided to remain in his

cell. This experience may have convinced Kevin that the time had now come for him to stay in this one place in the service of Christ.

Towards the end of his life, an angel appeared to Kevin once again and, after some discourse and a great deal of bargaining, led him to the place of his resurrection. It was during this discourse with the angel that a great prophecy was made about Glendalough.

The angel initially encouraged Kevin to go 'eastwards from the lesser lake'. When he hesitated, the angel insisted; 'If you go to the place indicated, many sons of light will always be in it and after your time the monks shall have a sufficiency of earthly possessions and many thousands of happy souls will arise with you from that place, to the kingdom of heaven'.[9] Then the angel promised Kevin that fifty monks would remain there after his death; Kevin demurred so the angel promised more; 'many thousands shall dwell there'. The angel also promised that after his resurrection, Kevin would still guide, influence and protect this community. Glendalough would remain sacred and venerable; 'kings and the powerful ones of Ireland shall honour it with a religious veneration on thy account. A great city shall spring up, and the ministry of thy monks shall be so perfect that none of them buried under the soil shall endure the pains of hell'.

The angel continued to make extravagant promises to Kevin, determined to encourage him to stay and spend the rest of his life in the valley. She even promised to 'make the mountains level' which Kevin refused, because of his concern for the animals that lived there. Eventually, legend insists, the angel and Kevin walked together upon the waters of the lake to the chosen place. Kevin seems to have questioned the wisdom of such a site, because it was rugged and in his opinion unsuitable for burials, but the angel insisted that the stones which had been immovable there since creation would now be movable. He finally said, 'In the name of our Lord Jesus Christ, arise with thy monks and go to that place, which the Lord hath ordained for thy resurrection'. After these words, the angel departed.

We are told that from his childhood to his declining years, Kevin always kept God's commandments, in holiness and justice. He was now approaching the final days of his life and he asked twelve of his monks to pray for a special intention. When their prayer was answered, he told them it was that he might be allowed to die. They felt sorrowful but he consoled them, saying that he had already been in God's kingdom on earth. He encouraged them to keep his Rule and all God's commandments. After this he raised his hands and blessed them and the place, and departed from them.

The legacy of St Kevin continues to weave through the lives and experiences, not only of those who visit Glendalough, but in a very real way through the stories and memories held by local people who live in this area. Kathleen Bolger (born 1909) who now lives in Laragh, is a surviving link of an old Glendalough family closely associated with the days when people went by boat to St Kevin's Bed. Her father, Edward, was born in the village at the upper end of the valley in 1874, where his father had worked before him in the mines. Her two brothers, her father and grandfather all made a part-time living on the lake, with two open rowing boats, taking people over to St Kevin's Bed and Templenaskellig. Her father and grandfather also provided the service of helping pilgrims to get into St Kevin's Bed, a dangerous and sometimes hazardous occupation. They were helped by Paddy Barrett and his son Paddy, who worked at St Kevin's Bed for forty seven years. However, it was Larry Bolger who rowed the last boat to St Kevin's Bed in 1965.

Kathleen lived all her life in the house on the lakeshore at the beginning of the Miner's Road. She remembers the crowds of people going to St Kevin's Bed, especially on Sundays and all through the summer. She recalls how it was very popular for newly married couples to go there on their wedding day. Many weddings were held at that time in the nearby Lake Hotel (now demolished). Kathleen herself only went to the Bed once in her lifetime, and says that was enough for her! She remembers that people first went to St Kevin's Bed where the tradition was to make three wishes having entered the cave. Afterwards they went to Templenaskellig, where they prayed in the old church. On returning to the far shore of the lake at the end of their journey, they could enjoy a cup of tea, scones and fresh-baked brown bread in Kathleen's house, for two shillings or ten new pence.

The stories and myths surrounding St Kevin can still fascinate and inspire us today, all these centuries later. They are soul-full, curious and magical; full of dark and light, mists and moments of great clarity; tangible and yet intangible. They are archetypal stories. We all fight the 'monsters of the deep'; we all struggle with conflicts and contradictory longings that pull us at times in different directions. There is still so much in Kevin's story that remains unexplored. Perhaps as we touch into his experience and walk in his footsteps, Kevin's story may help us to understand more of our own story, his struggles illuminate our own struggles, the peace he found become our peace. May his dream give us hope and courage to follow our own dreams, as we make our pilgrimage through the valley.

Trinity Church

I feel stones remortared with love
Preserving, protecting
A reminder of a people, their dreams
founded on love and things sacred
I stand in awe between rolling hills
A pilgrim, I walk slowly, searching, seeking
Finding that deep peace
and a sense of God.
(A recent pilgrim to Glendalough)

Trinity Church is a beautifully simple and well-preserved example of an early Irish nave and chancel church. According to John O'Donovan, 'It is the most curious and of its age the most perfect specimen of an ancient Irish *Daimhliag* (stone church)'.[1] It was built in the eleventh century, probably on the site of an older church made of wood, dating back to the sixth or seventh century. It is easy to miss this church on a visit to Glendalough because, like St Saviour's and St Mary's Church, it lies outside the main monastic enclosure in a secluded position, on the southern side of the road to Laragh, two hundred meters from the entrance to the OPW Centre and car park (*see map, p 43*). In 1873 Sir William Wilde attributed the well-preserved state of this church to the fact that there were no burials there and it did not form part of the route for pilgrims.[2]

The stile which leads to the church can be found by the sign for Trinity Church on the main road. After climbing down some stone steps, the north wall of the nave of the church immediately catches the eye. This old wall has character and coherence and the stones have not moved since they were placed here almost a thousand years ago.

Nearly all the stones in the wall are mica schist, the ancient rock of the valley which is over five hundred million years old. Some of the stones, especially in the lower part of the walls, are quite large and laid in a horizontal position. It has been said that stones are tabernacles of memory. If these stones could speak, what a story they might tell.

Walking around the outside of the church, it is noticeable that there is a large granite stone at the foundation of each corner of the nave. There are also a few granite stones including one very large one that seems to be out of place in the south wall. Did the builders include these stones in appreciation of the great granite boulders scattered throughout the valley since the Ice Age ended ten thousand years ago? The granite is fifty million years younger than the mica schist and comes from the heart of the Wicklow Mountains, which is exposed at the upper end of the Glendalough valley.

Before entering the church it is well worth walking around the outside of the building first, in order to appreciate the character and spirit of this place and to make contact in your own imagination with those who lived and worshipped here in the past. As we look beyond the outer walls in all directions, this is a good place to reflect on why we have come to Glendalough on pilgrimage, who we are and where we have come from.

As we enter the church through the doorway in the south wall, the chancel arch is the first outstanding, visible feature. It is beautiful in its simplicity, just over three meters high and about three meters wide. In 1873 Sir William Wilde described this arch as one of the finest of its kind in Ireland. On the side facing the nave, there are fifteen granite stones almost equal in size with a keystone in the centre which has slipped slightly. Is there a special significance in the fact that there are seven stones on either side of the keystone? Seven is a sacred number signifying wholeness

and completion. The keystone holds the balance in the structure
of the arch. Here, we might reflect on what is the keystone of our
lives and how we hold the balance between the good and bad,
the light and the dark of life's experiences.

On the opposite side of the arch, facing the east window, there
are fourteen similar, well-shaped granite stones. There are six
stones in the arch of the beautiful chancel window in the gable
facing east. Turning from the chancel arch towards the west, in
the centre of the western gable we can admire one of Glendalough's most remarkable doorways. Like Reefert, Templenaskellig and St Mary's, this door is in the semi-cyclopean style
with a square head and sloping jambs. It is built with seven large
stones of hand-cut granite with a massive lintel on top. This
powerfully built doorway, in such a simple church, must have

Trinity Church Doorway

had a very special significance for those who built it. Do the seven stones beneath the lintel represent the seven stages of life?

Is the doorway a symbol of the connection between the outer and inner worlds, the place where the two become one? It is good to focus what is going on in our outer world from within our inner being. We need a sacred space in order to do that. Christ stands at the doorway and invites us to make the connection through him. 'I am the door; whoever enters through me will be safe, he will go in and out and find pasture' (Jn 10:9).

The doorway in the southern wall, with its round-headed arch, was added to the building when the western annex was built. On the same wall there is a window, deeply splayed on the inside and semi-circular at the top. There is also a very beautiful, small, triangular-headed window in the southern wall of the chancel. The annex is a very unusual feature in this type of church. It is almost square, measuring approximately three meters by three meters. There was once a round tower (*cloigtheach*) built on this square base which was eighteen meters high and almost three meters in diameter.

An eighteenth century drawing showing the round tower

In 1818 it collapsed in a storm along with the south and west walls of the annex. The walls were rebuilt but the tower was never restored. The north wall with its window is therefore the most authentic and original wall of the annex. The north window is very attractive, with a barely discernible Celtic cross on the sill stone.

The church is called Trinity Church but this was probably not its original name. It is sometimes linked to a saint called Mac Cuaroc, who is said to have ministered the last rites to St Kevin when he died. The Trinity always held a central place in Irish spirituality. Before Christianity came to Ireland there was a tendency to triplicate in the old religion and Patrick seems to have made good use of this in confession of the Trinity. A strong belief in the Trinity was incorporated into many of the ancient hymns and prayers. In a very simple way, people accepted the Triune God, as in the saying, 'three folds in a cloth, three joints in a finger, three leaves in a shamrock; frost, snow, ice, all of them water, three persons in God also.' There is a prayer in Irish which was said for protection throughout the day:

> Athair, Mac is Spiorad Naomh,
> Bíodh an Triúr-in-Aon linn lá is oíche,
> Ar chúl na dtonn nó ar thaobh na mbeann,
> Bíodh ár Máthair linn is a lámh um ár gceann.

> Father, Son and Holy Spirit
> May the Three-in-One be with us day and night,
> In the depths of the waves and on the sides of the mountains,
> May our Mother be with us with her arm around our heads.

A strong belief in the Trinity and faith in its protective power is nowhere more apparent than in the great Celtic hymn known as St Patrick's Breastplate. Whilst this hymn cannot be traced before the eighth century, its origins could date to the time of St Patrick in the fifth century or even earlier. There are many breastplate prayers from that earlier time. Noel Dermot O'Donoghue comments on the significance of this hymn for us today: 'One thing is certain, the breastplate, as it has come down to us, is a messenger from a world at once familiar and strange, a messenger that is put in question by our contemporary sense or senses of the meaning of Christianity, but also a messenger that puts our contemporary understanding of Christianity in question, and may well have much to say to us that can illuminate our journey into the future.'[3]

There is a story told about Kevin and his monks, related to the praying of St Patrick's Breastplate. Perhaps it even happened in this church?

> On a certain night, St Kevin and his monks were engaged singing a hymn to St Patrick. Suddenly, the holy abbot remained in a silent ecstasy and then ordered his brothers to sing this hymn three times. When the monks asked why they should sing it so often, the abbot said, 'Our holy patron Patrick, whose hymn you have sung, stood on the pavement, leaning on his staff and he blessed us, when we ceased our singing.[4]

The hymn begins by calling on the great name of the Trinity: 'For my shield this day I call a mighty power: the Holy Trinity'.[5] The prayer then introduces the power of Christ, who lived among us and rose again for our salvation. It gathers together the powers of heaven and earth, centred in the strength and wisdom of God, to protect us from fears and the dangers that threaten us. When the evils that threaten us are exposed and acknowledged by name, there is a wonderful sense of freedom in the prayer; we feel more able to trust in the all-pervasive presence of Christ. The Christ of this prayer is a tender, loving, cosmic presence; always with us and watching over us. This is a Christ who is close to us in a relationship of love.

We leave Trinity Church impressed by its endurance and openness. The open doors, windows and roof speak a message for today's rapidly changing world. Are they asking us to be open to all the new movements of the Spirit alive in our age, at the

same time reminding us not to forget the rich treasures of the
past? This church was built around the beginning of this millennium. Its enduring presence fills us with hope as we prepare to
open the door to a new era.

St Patrick's Breastplate

For my shield this day I call:
A mighty power:
The Holy Trinity!
Affirming threeness,
Confessing oneness,
in the making of all
Through love …

For my shield this day I call:
Christ's power in his coming
and in his baptising,
Christ's power in his dying
On the cross, his arising
from the tomb, his ascending;
Christ's power in his coming
for judgement and ending.

For my shield this day I call:
strong power of the seraphim,
with angels obeying,
and archangels attending,
in the glorious company
of the holy and risen ones,
in the prayers of the fathers,
in visions prophetic
and commands apostolic
in the annals of witness …

For my shield this day I call:
Heaven's might,
sun's brightness,
Moon's whiteness,

Fire's glory,
Lightning's swiftness,
Wind's wildness,
Ocean's depth
Earth's solidity,
Rock's immobility.

This day I call to me:
God's strength to direct me,
God's power to sustain me,
God's wisdom to guide me,
God's vision to light me,
God's ear to my hearing,
God's word to my speaking,
God's hand to uphold me,
God's pathway before me,
God's shield to protect me ...
from evil enticements,
from failings of nature,
from one man or many,
that seek to destroy me,
anear or afar ...

Around me I gather
these forces to save
my soul and my body ...

against knowledge unlawful
that injures the body,
that injures the spirit.

Be Christ this day my strong protector,
against poison and burning,
against drowning and wounding,
through reward wide and plenty ...

Christ beside me, Christ before me;
Christ behind me, Christ within me;
Christ beneath me, Christ above me;
Christ to right of me, Christ to left of me;
Christ in my lying, my sitting, my rising;
Christ in heart of all who know me;
Christ on tongue of all who meet me;
Christ in eye of all who see me;
Christ in ear of all who hear me.

For my shield this day I call
a mighty power:
the Holy Trinity!
affirming threeness,
confessing oneness
in the making of all
through love ...
(Translation by Noel Dermot O'Donoghue)

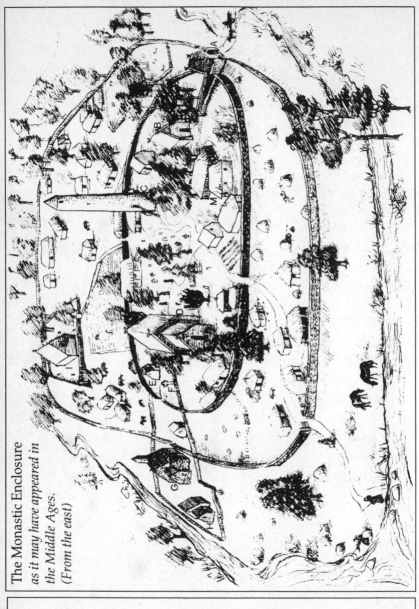

The Monastic Enclosure
as it may have appeared in
the Middle Ages.
(From the east)

Key

A Gateway

B North church

C Round Tower

D Cathedral

E Priest's House

F St Kevin's
Cross

G St Kevin's
church

H St Kieran's
church

I St Mary's
church

M Guest houses

The Monastic City

Glendalough is a holy place and was probably a religious centre before the arrival of Christianity in Ireland in the fourth century C.E. It has been called a liminal place – where earth and heaven seem to meet and there is a sense that God is not far away. For three thousand years before Christianity came to Ireland, circular stone walls with standing stones (such as Newgrange in Co Meath) or wooden enclosures (such as Tara) were erected to denote the boundaries of a sacred enclosure. Here, sacred rituals and burials took place and there was a profound awareness of the presence of the otherworld. Ancient standing stones had great spiritual significance as the *axis mundi* or axis of the world – energy lines which connected heaven and earth. The Christian monastery was a new sacred place and the circular walls witnessed to that powerful continuation of cultic and religious beliefs which had always existed in Irish society. In the Golden Age of Celtic Christianity (450-1050 CE), the fires of ancient beliefs and practices were rekindled and transformed by those who flocked to the churches and rural monasteries in response to the calling of Christ.

Glendalough was known as 'The Monastic City' and is a typical example of an early Celtic monastery. It provided a sanctuary for expression of the deepest and most vibrant religious and spiritual beliefs of the people and a place where the veil between this world and the next was perceived to be only wafer thin.

It is a paradox that such small, isolated rural monasteries were called monastic 'cities', especially in Ireland where there were no urban centres. The Roman concept of a city was adapted by the desert monks in Egypt, Syria and Palestine in the fourth century to denote a monastic settlement in the wilderness. This was a deliberate way of showing how desert monasteries differed from the secular cities. The monastic 'cities' were places under the rule of God where the kingdom of God was made manifest; its citizens were not citizens of Rome, but citizens of heaven. The fact that Glendalough was called the Monastic City underlines the great connection between early Celtic monasticism and the desert spiritual traditions of the eastern orthodox churches.[1]

The Gateway to the Monastic City marked the boundary between the secular world outside and the sacred space within, where the rule of God was respected and those seeking refuge could find shelter. It was a healing sanctuary, often associated with miracles and cures for the sick. An ultimate sense of healing came through death, which was always referred to as the place of resurrection. The cemetery was a very special place in the early monasteries and could usually be found within the walls of the sanctuary, marking the place of transition from this world to the next.

Inside the Monastic City, all the activities of an early Irish monastery would have taken place, including writing and the illumination of manuscripts, monastic training, education, agriculture, silverwork, metalwork, tanning and other crafts and activities linked to the provision of hospitality. Buildings would have included the bakery, kitchen, tannery, infirmary, refectory, scriptorium, library, accommodation for visitors and students and residential quarters for the monks. Large monastic cities like Glendalough had two enclosures. The central enclosure included some of the most impressive buildings such as the cathedral, abbot's house, guest houses and the round tower. Other residential houses, cells and churches were located within the outer enclosure of the monastery (*see map, p 38*).

One of the strong attractions of early Celtic monasticism is that it was an inclusive Christian community. There was probably a non-clerical atmosphere about the place, as most monks were lay people, and men, women and children would all have lived within the sanctuary of the monastery. Life in the Monastic City was therefore very different from the separatist and more exclusive orders which developed in Europe after the twelfth century.

Glendalough had a special reputation as a place of scholarship and learning. According to Wright, 'a seminary was founded from which many saints were sent forth whose sanctity and learning diffused around the western world'.[2] It is possible that some ancient manuscripts were written here, including the manuscript known as Rawlinson B 502 (The Book of Glendalough) which may have been written by scribes in the Monastic City.[3]

Glendalough also gained a great reputation as a pilgrimage centre during the so-called Dark Ages (600-1000 CE) after the collapse of the Roman Empire, when the pilgrim roads to Rome and the Holy Land were closed or unsafe. It became famous as one of the four great pilgrimage centres in Ireland, together with Croagh Patrick, Loch Derg and Skellig Michael. Aengus, an eighth century Irish bard and member of the Céile Dé, called Glendalough 'The Rome of the western world'. It was said that, 'seven pilgrimages to Glendalough were as valuable as one to Rome'.

In the tenth century, at the height of its fame and fortune, the Monastic City may have attracted visitors and pilgrims from all Ireland, Britain and Europe. Pilgrimages took place throughout the year but especially on the Pattern Day or Feast of Glendalough's patron saint, St Kevin, on June 3rd. The Pattern Day Pilgrimage ended in the 1860s because of disorderly behaviour. This was unacceptable to the Catholic Church which was growing in power and influence at that time.

The existence of such an extensive infrastructure for pilgrimage at Glendalough raises the question as to whether the Monastic City, with its seven ancient churches, was developed essentially for pilgrimage purposes when it was restored during the tenth and eleventh centuries during a significant period of revival in the Celtic tradition. Glendalough has never been systematically excavated, and without further archaeological and historical research it is impossible to estimate its full significance and purpose both as a Celtic monastery and a national centre of pilgrimage. One thing is certain. Glendalough once shone like a jewel in the crown of Celtic monasticism, together with Kildare, Clonmacnoise, Bangor, Kells, Iona, Inismor and many other great monasteries which flourished during the so called 'Golden Age' when Celtic Christianity brought inspiration and guidance to an uncertain and changing Europe.

We recommend visiting the main monuments of the Monastic City in the way of a pilgrim, stopping at the various places we have called stations. We suggest first passing through the Gateway near the Glendalough Hotel, as this is the ancient entrance to the Monastic City.

Once inside the inner enclosure, the most obvious building is the Round Tower. The next is the Cathedral with its ancient cemetery which encloses the little building known as the Priest's House. St Kevin's Cross stands in what remains of the wall of the old cemetery. In the outer enclosure, the churches of St Kevin and St Kieran are very near. St Mary's Church is further away and is not so accessible (*see map, p 43*). These stations can be visited in any order which suits the individual visitor.

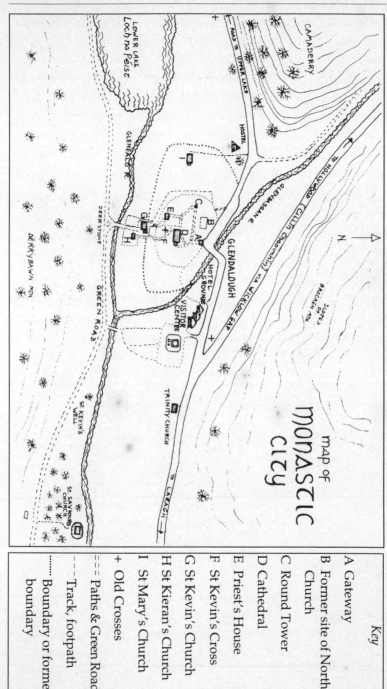

map of
monastic
city

Key

A Gateway
B Former site of North Church
C Round Tower
D Cathedral
E Priest's House
F St Kevin's Cross
G St Kevin's Church
H St Kieran's Church
I St Mary's Church
+ Old Crosses
=== Paths & Green Road
- - - Track, footpath
...... Boundary or former boundary

The Gateway

The fortress of Eamhan Macha has vanished
except that its stones remain.
The Monastic City of the western world
Is Glendalough of the Assemblies.
(*Féilire of Oengus*, c. 800 CE)

The Gateway marked the main entrance to the old monastery of
Glendalough and is the only one of its kind surviving in Ireland.
It was probably built into the great stone wall or *caiseal* which
once surrounded the Monastic City. The gateway has double
archways over a flagged causeway which can still be seen on the

path inside the gate. It is likely that the corbel stones that jut out of the side walls between the arches supported a roof or floor of an upper chamber. This room was probably the gatekeeper's house. Just inside the gate, on the wall on the right hand side of the path, there is a great slab of mica schist, with a cross incised on it. This cross probably marked the point of entrance into the monastery for a refugee.

The gateway had a very special significance, the threshold or entrance into the sanctuary. In the Celtic tradition such places were often marked with special stones or crosses. The monasteries were set apart and respected as places of sanctuary whose boundaries should not be violated. Refugees, prisoners, even criminals or those fleeing any kind of danger or difficulty, could be granted protection at the monastery. This custom was valued in what was often a turbulent society, and served to fulfil the religious duties of the monks, whilst bringing people under the control of the monastic authorities.[4]

For a pilgrim visiting Glendalough today, the moment of entering through the gateway can be a very special experience, evoking thoughts of sanctuary and sacred space. The word sanctuary is derived from the Latin word *sanctus*, meaning holy. Passing through the gateway of Glendalough, we are entering holy ground. The Gateway to the Monastic City marks an entrance to refuge and an opening to new experience. The best time to visit for quietness and prayer is early morning or late evening. We invite you to walk slowly and reverently through this sacred place and reflect on the kind of sanctuary or new experience you may wish to find here.

> *Psalm 24*
> The earth is the Lord's and all that is in it,
> the world, and those who live in it;
> for he has founded it on the seas,
> and established it on the rivers.
>
> Who shall ascend the hill of the Lord?
> And who shall stand in his holy place?
> Those who have clean hands and pure hearts,
> who do not lift up their souls to what is false,
> and do not swear deceitfully.
>
> They will receive blessing from the Lord,
> and vindication from the God of their salvation.
> Such is the company of those who seek him,
> who seek the face of the God of Jacob.
>
> Lift up your heads, O gates!
> and be lifted up, O ancient doors!
> that the King of glory may come in.

The Round Tower

The Round Tower is one of the best known early symbols of the Irish Church. These unique structures are found mainly in Ireland, a few in Scotland and one in the Isle of Man. There are sixty-five round towers surviving, in whole or in part, throughout Ireland.[5]

The Irish name for the round tower is *cloigtheach* which means bell house and this suggests an original use as bell towers. They did not have hanging bells as in the modern church steeples, so if they were used as bell towers the bell was probably rung by hand through one of the windows near the top of the tower. It has been suggested the towers were used as storehouses for the monastic treasures with one of the most important of these being the monastery bell. Perhaps that is where the name *cloigtheach* comes from.

There is also a popular belief that the towers were built for refuge when the monastery came under attack and that would explain why the door is placed four meters above ground level, so that the ladder used to gain entry could be removed once people were safely inside. The windows near the top look out in all directions, covering every approach road. Perhaps the tower was used as a lookout. It is interesting to note that the Round Tower of Glendalough has seven storeys. This number always had special significance in religious tradition. It raises the question as to whether the round towers were also used for prayer and sacred purposes.

There has been much debate about the meaning and purpose of the round towers. Perhaps they were simply built to give glory to God and witness to the faith of the monastic community for everybody to see. Certainly they must have been a very welcome sight to weary travellers and pilgrims as they approached the end of their journey, looking for sanctuary and shelter for the night.

Glendalough's round tower is one of the finest in Ireland. It is just over thirty meters high, built on a meter of foundations that are placed directly on the subsoil. The walls are about one meter thick at the bottom and taper slightly all the way to the top. The diameter of the tower is about five meters at the base narrowing to just over four meters at the beginning of the conical roof. This roof collapsed at some stage but it was restored in 1876 using the original stones that had fallen inside the tower.

The doorway is four meters from the ground and the first floor is inside the sill of the doorway. Below the first floor there is a basement, and above it, five other floors with one small window lighting each storey, apart from the top floor which has four windows. The windows are square-headed and taper slightly like the tower itself. The doorway is built of granite stones with inclined jambs capped by a single granite stone with a round head cut in it. This indicates that Glendalough's round tower is not among the earliest in Ireland which have square-headed doorways. It was probably built in the late tenth or early eleventh century.

Ireland's round towers remain today as a powerful symbol of the courage and conviction of those who built them and their determination to resist whatever threatened that faith. Like the famous High Crosses which can be found at Monasterboice and throughout Ireland, the round towers stood as witness to faith and helped to communicate it for all to see.

The Round Tower is a symbol of faith, determination, welcome and safety. As we stand here, we can ask what faith means to us today, as we approach the beginning of the third millennium. What values do we uphold and defend, and what monuments to our faith are we leaving behind for future generations to question or admire? We invite you to walk slowly around the tower, touching its walls and feeling the encircling presence and protective power of God.

Psalm 61:1-3

Hear my cry, O God;
listen to my prayer.
From the end of the earth I call to you
when my heart is faint.
Lead me to the rock that is higher than I;
for you are my refuge,
a strong tower against the enemy.

An early Irish bronze bell

The Cathedral

The Cathedral is the largest of Glendalough's old churches. The nave is fifteen meters long and nine meters wide, which is perhaps the widest of all early Irish Churches. It was dedicated to St Peter and St Paul and was the Cathedral Church until Glendalough was joined with the Archdiocese of Dublin in 1214.

The oldest part of the building dates from the late tenth or early eleventh centuries. This is best seen in the west gable, up to the top of the doorway, and in the north and south walls up to a height of about one meter. The great slabs of mica schist that are used in this part of the building are not as solid as they look. They are like large flagstones laid on their sides on the inside and outside of the wall, with the space in between filled with rubble.

Above the large stones the second phase of building can be seen. It is a very different type of masonry using much smaller stones. This work may have been completed after the original building was destroyed. All that remains of the chancel arch, the chancel itself and the north doorway, were probably added in the twelfth century. By the time repair work was carried out from 1875-79, the building was in a very ruined state. During the restoration, the piers and arches of the chancel were rebuilt using what was left of the original stones.

The most noteworthy features of the nave as it now stands are the west doorway, the south windows and the remains of both the north doorway and the chancel arch. The west doorway is built with local mica schist. It is an old trabeate doorway with the jambs leaning a little from sill to lintel in the old Irish style of building. Above the lintel stone there is an arch built in the wall, as in St Kevin's Church. This is a supporting arch which takes the weight of the huge gable off the lintel stone; it is known as a semi-cyclopean arch. There are two plain, unadorned, round-headed windows in the south wall.

Another notable feature in the nave of the cathedral can be seen from the outside. These are the corner antae or extensions of the north and south walls, extending beyond the gables. These were probably constructed to support the heavy external roof trusses. The chancel itself was built at the same time as the chancel arch in the twelfth century. It measures approximately eleven meters by four meters and is built in poor quality masonry. It originally had four windows, two in the north wall and one in the south wall which were never rebuilt. The fourth window in the east gable is tall and round-headed with chevron decoration. South of the chancel there is a small room, which was the sacristy of the cathedral. This room had its own exit door facing east.

The Cathedral was at the centre of the Monastic City, a place where the monks sought to unite themselves on this earth to the one God. It would have held a different atmosphere to the smaller and more secluded or contemplative churches by the Upper Lake. Daily life was organised around the three central activities of prayer, labour and study, but for the monk the highest form of prayer was the Divine Office. This would have taken place in the Cathedral which was the centre of all formal liturgy and worship.

The Divine Office consisted of eight hours or prayer times. Many of these services included the cross vigil, a penitential way of praying with arms outstretched. Hymns, psalms and canticles were said or sung throughout the day and night, especially the *Magnificat* or Song of Mary, the *Benedictus* and the Canticle of the Three Young Men. Two monks kept vigil in the church throughout the night, reciting the psalter. Long hours of prayer were acceptable to the Irish who favoured vocal prayers and external practices. Scripture, and especially the gospel of St John and the letters of St Paul, were favourite readings.[6] The penitential nature of monastic discipline and the difficulties of going to church early on a cold, wet and windy morning, is clear from the following poem which was written about Glendalough:

The wind o'er the Hog's Back moans
It takes the trees and lays them low,
And shivering monks o'er frozen stones
To the twin hours of night-time go.[7]

This is a place to imagine what the celebration of worship was like in the Cathedral, with the monks making their way from their cells to fulfil their obligations and monastic duties. Whilst the Cathedral now stands in ruins, we can imagine the atmosphere when it was echoing with the sound of the monks singing, the smell of incense burning and the magnificence of beautiful metalwork and illuminated manuscripts used for worship and the Divine Office.

The Cathedral stands witness to a noble attempt by a community to live in a way that would 'unite themselves on this earth to one God'. Here we can reflect for a moment on the world we live in and ask ourselves how we may encourage a communion with others which strives towards a common ideal. How can we unite ourselves with God and with each other in the world we live in?

Psalm 119 is the longest psalm in the bible. It was very popular in the monastic church:

Happy are those whose way is blameless,
who walk in the law of the Lord.
Happy are those who keep his decrees
who seek him with their whole heart,
who also do no wrong,
but walk in his ways.

You have commanded your precepts
to be kept diligently.
O that my ways may be steadfast
in keeping your statutes!
Then I shall not be put to shame,
having my eyes fixed on all
your commandments.

I will praise you with an upright heart,
when I learn your righteous ordinances.
I will observe your statutes;
do not utterly forsake me.

The Priest's House and the Cemetery

You must teach your children that the ground
beneath their feet is the ashes of their ancestors.
(The Great Chief Sends Word)

A monastic settlement was never complete without its cemetery, and at Glendalough this is situated near the south west corner of the cathedral. This cemetery stands as a testament to the many lives woven into the fabric of Glendalough's history; but perhaps even more it reminds us of our time of transition from this world to the next. Sunset is a magical time to visit this place; a time when day moves almost imperceptibly into night, as one day we will move from this life to the next.

The remains of the walls of the old cemetery can still be seen, roughly quadrangular in shape. One wall ran southwards from the cathedral for thirty meters. St Kevin's Cross stood in the middle of this wall. Another wall ran due west from the cathedral for thirty meters. Within the old cemetery stands the ruins of an unusual building known as The Priest's House. The fact that this building stood within the grounds of the ancient cemetery led to speculation that it may have covered the grave of St Kevin himself or housed his relics. It has also been suggested that it was a mortuary chapel for the monastery.

The name 'Priest's House' comes from more recent times when local priests were buried there. The graves of two priests in particular who died in the eighteenth century, and who had reputations as healers in their lifetime, were the object of special interest from visitors and pilgrims. Clay was taken from their graves and miracles were attributed to the application of this clay, accompanied by prayers, reminiscent of the miracle performed by Jesus (Jn 9:6).

There is a recess in the interior of the west wall, just inside the narrow doorway. The lintel of this doorway contains an unusual carved stone. Beranger found this stone on the ground at the Priest's Church in 1779 and made a drawing of it. This shows a seated ecclesiastic or monk flanked by a bowing figure on the right holding what appears to be a bell, together with a kneeling figure on the left holding a staff or crozier. According to Wilde, 'There can be little doubt that this is the oldest sculptured stone in Glendalough and is probably one of the oldest incised stones in Ireland'.[8] It is very unlikely that this stone was originally in the lintel of the doorway, where it can now be found. It could have been part of a cross or gravestone.

Beranger's drawing of the east end of the Priest's House

The most remarkable feature of the Priest's House is the recessed arch in the eastern gable. This was incorrectly reconstructed in 1875-79 following a drawing by George Petrie. There was an older drawing made by Beranger in 1779 which clearly shows that the arch did not have a wall built into it as it does today. Very little of what Beranger saw remains today. The partly reconstructed arch contains thirteen of the original carved stones or *voussoirs*. It is likely that in the original building this arch contained either a window or a door leading in to the building.

Because it was believed that the Priest's House contained the relics of St Kevin, it became a very special place for pilgrims to visit. Visitors did not go inside, but put a piece of cloth through the window to touch the relics. This cloth would then be used for healing. The Priest's House was an important place for pilgrims to visit on the Feast of St Kevin until quite recently. People first went to St Kevin's Well and then to the Priest's House where they collected some clay to bring home for healing purposes.

The Cemetery continues to be used for burials today by members of the local Catholic parish of Glendalough and Laragh. Visitors are often drawn to explore the inscriptions and decorations on the gravestones. The Cemetery is a place which reminds us of our own mortality and the fact that we too will eventually be laid to rest. It provides an opportunity to reflect on our life, death and resurrection and consider what special healing we may wish to ask for, both for ourselves and for others.

> Who's afraid of death? I think that only fools are. For it is not as though this thing were given to one man only, but all receive it. The journey that my friend makes, I can make also. If I know nothing else, I know this, I go where he is. O fools, shrinking from that little door, through which so many kind and lovely souls have passed before you, will you hang back? Harder in your case than another? Not so. And too much silence? Has there not been enough stir here? Go bravely, for where so much greatness and gentleness have been already, you should be glad to follow.

(Monk Gibbon, from *The Tremulous String*)

Beranger's drawing of the stone from the Priest's House

St Kevin's Cross

High Crosses are amongst the best known and most powerful symbols of early Celtic Christianity. They are found throughout the Celtic world but the greatest number survive in Ireland, where more than sixty still remain largely intact. There are remnants of more than a hundred other crosses, and it is suggested that there were hundreds more which have now completely disappeared. The oldest cross dates to the eighth century, and by the thirteenth century every monastery had its cross. Glendalough had many ancient crosses, the most notable survivors being St Kevin's Cross which now stands in the cemetery near the Cathedral, and the Market Cross which can be found displayed in the exhibition room at the Visitors' Centre.

Detail from the Market Cross

The most distinctive feature of the Celtic Cross is the ring which encircles the top of the shaft and arms. The idea for this may have come from the Middle East and Egypt where circular wreaths were often placed around the arms of the cross, symbolising Christ's victory over death. It was the sculpting of the rings in stone which made the Celtic Crosses so unique. Some people see no more significance in the ring than a structural design to support the heavy arms of the cross, preventing them from breaking. However, pilgrims believe that these special features hold deep religious and spiritual significance.

There are three main types of Celtic crosses found in Ireland. First are plain crosses, of which St Kevin's Cross in the cemetery at Glendalough is a very good example. This cross was carved from a single granite stone about three meters high and over one meter across the arms.[9] The ring of this cross is unusual because it is not perforated right through at the intersection of the upright and the arms.

The second main type of cross found in Ireland is the ornamental cross. The best example of this type is at Ahenny in County Tipperary. It is elaborately decorated with abstract interlacing patterns carved on the stone. This type of decoration can be seen on the back and sides of the Market Cross in Glendalough and also on the cross standing in the south west corner of the graveyard at Reefert Church, by the Upper Lake.

The most well-known style of Celtic cross is not found in Glendalough at all. These are the scriptural crosses with carved figures representing biblical themes and stories arranged around the central figure of the crucified and risen Christ. Robin Flower, who lived in the Blasket Islands, once described these crosses as 'sermons in stone'. The best known scriptural crosses in Ireland are Muiredach's Cross at Monasterboice, about fifty kilometers north of Dublin, and the Cross of the Scriptures at Clonmacnoise, on the banks of the River Shannon. Muiredach's Cross dates from the early tenth century.[10]

In the twelfth century, when the old monastic Church began to decline and a diocesan organisation was more firmly established, the carved figures on the crosses told the story of these changes and the reforming of monastic structures. Christ is shown as usual in the central position but below him now stands the figure of a robed ecclesiastic. Placing the bishop in a prominent position obviously underlined his new role and authority in the Church, significantly replacing the figures of the lay abbots and pilgrims shown on previous carvings we have mentioned. The Market Cross in Glendalough is a good example of this later type of Celtic cross, which is also found at Kilfenora and Dysert O'Dea in County Clare. Many of these crosses lack the earlier and distinctive ring shape.

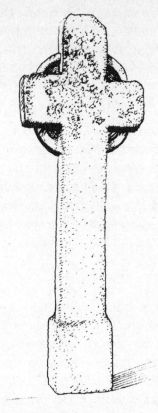

St Kevin's Cross

The high crosses were used to mark sacred boundary places and were usually placed outside the main church in the monastery. People gathered around the crosses, which provided powerful aids for preaching and teaching, not just to those who could not read the scriptures in Latin, but to all who were inspired and humbled by them. They have continued through the centuries to be symbols of faith, and were often visited by people for prayers during the Penal and Famine times.

What is the religious significance of the circle around the cross? Perhaps it suggests a connection with pre-Christian sun worship, marking the sign of the cross against the circle of the sun. The circle is a symbol of eternity and God who is without beginning or end. The cross is a symbol of salvation and the great victory of life over death through the resurrection of Christ. The cross and circle together are a reminder of the eternal work of God in creation. Esther de Waal writes, 'Whatever its origins, there is no doubt that the symbolism of the circle of creation held in tension with the cross of redemption makes a very powerful impression on anyone who today stands in front of one of these crosses'.[11]

The two central pillars of faith and teaching in the Celtic tradition concerned creation and redemption. People had a keen sense of God's presence and power in creation and a real appreciation of life as a gift. They also had a profound awareness of evil and sin and acknowledged the need for protection and salvation. Celtic Christianity was therefore very often a spirituality of struggle; Christ was venerated as one who overcame evil by dying and rising from the dead.

In the Celtic understanding of God there is a connection between the human and the divine, time and eternity. Every daily activity and journey was marked by the sign of blessing and preservation. The sign of the cross was used for protection and for the commendation to God of all thoughts, activities and decisions. Even when situations went wrong, people were able to see their misfortune as less than the suffering of Christ. The following maxim may often have been heard on their lips, 'Ba mhó páis Chríost ná é' (The Passion of Christ was more than that). While emphasising the triumph of life over death in the resurrection of Christ, the Celtic Churches strongly identified with the sufferings endured on the cross. There were, for example, many poems and hymns in old Irish concerning the Passion and death of Christ, which incorporated a deep feeling towards the suffering he endured and a desire to become one with its healing power:

O King of the Friday
Whose limbs were stretched on the cross
O Lord who didst suffer
The bruises, the wounds, the loss.

We stretch ourselves
Beneath the shield of thy might
May some fruit from the tree of thy passion
Fall on us this night.
(Version by Douglas Hyde)

There is a traditional local belief that a person who can stand
with their back to St Kevin's cross, stretching their arms behind
them until their fingers touch, will have their wish granted. Why
not join your arms around the cross, perhaps with someone else,
in a gesture known as 'hugging the cross', and focus your spiritual intentions for a moment in silence and prayer. What is your
wish?

The Eternal Cross

He'll blossom on the cross in three weeks now
The saviour of the world will die again.
He is the flower upon a hurting bough,
The crown of thorns and nails will give him pain
But the worst one is how

We go on daily wounding him and he,
Although he's out of time, still feels the great
Dark of betrayal. He's nailed on a tree
Each time we fail him. Suffering won't abate
Until the liberty

This God-Man gave us is used only for
Kindness and gentleness. Our world is full
Of dying Christs – the starved, the sick, the poor.
God sleeps in cardboard boxes, has no meal.
We are his torturer

Each time we fail in generosity,
Abuse a child or will not give our love.
Christ lets us use our fatal liberty
Against himself. But now and then one move
of selflessness sets free

The whole of mankind whom he saw at play
And work as he hung dying, when his side
Was pierced. That spear was how we fail to say
We love someone, but each time tears are dried
It's Resurrection Day.

Elizabeth Jennings (*Times and Seasons*)

The Market Cross

St Kevin's Church

From all that dwells below the skies
Let faith and hope and joy arise
Let beauty, truth and good be sung
Through every land, by every tongue.
(Unitarian Prayer)

Apart from the Round Tower, St Kevin's Church is probably the best known monument in Glendalough. It is a unique building in which a small round tower is combined with a church.

There is a similar building with a stone roof about the same age in Kells, County Meath which is known as St Colm's House, but this does not have a round tower built into it. The round tower looks like a chimney built into the western gable of St Kevin's Church and has given it the popular name of St Kevin's House or St Kevin's Kitchen. St Kevin's Church was probably built in the late tenth century with the extensions being completed one or two hundred years later.

The original church was one room, measuring approximately seven meters by four meters. The walls are more than a meter thick and slope inwards slightly in the style of old Irish stone buildings. The roof is built with corbelled stones and pitched steeply to allow the water to drain easily. Each layer of stones overlaps the previous layer slightly as it slopes inwards, rising towards the ridge of the roof. The use of corbelling shows that this effective method of dry stone roofing continued in Ireland long after the same basic techniques were used at Newgrange two thousand years before. Where the inward corbelling reduced the distance between the two sides of the roof to two meters, an arch was built for additional structural support. The arch can be seen clearly from inside the church. Above this arch there is a small open space known as a croft. It is no more than one and a half meters high in the centre but it could have been used for sleeping. There is a small window facing east which lights this croft.

Below the vault there was an apartment directly over the church on the ground floor. The large beams which supported the floor of this apartment were set in the church walls, about four meters from the ground. Most of the holes into which the beams were set can still be seen. The apartment was just over two meters high under the top of the arch and it extended for the full length of the church. It was lit by a window facing east. Access was gained probably by a ladder from the church through an opening in the floor.

St Kevin's Church originally had no chancel or adjoining sacristy. The doorway in the western gable is about two meters high with a lintel which is a single large stone of local mica schist. Above the lintel there is a supporting arch of granite stones in the semi-cyclopean style similar to that above the cathedral door. There are two holes in the lintel stone, indicating that the original door hung from the lintel like a shutter which was opened by lifting upwards. In the jambs of the doorway there is a mixture of local granite and mica schist. There were two windows in the original church, neither of which survived changes and renovations. There was a small window in the south wall which was removed to make way for a bigger window, in the early part of the nineteenth century, when the church was used by the local Roman Catholics to celebrate Sunday Mass. That window was subsequently closed. The east window was removed when the chancel was added and a chancel arch had to be broken through the east wall.

The single stone of the arch of the old east window can still be seen, just above the top of this chancel arch. The chancel itself was still standing in 1722 but now it has completely disappeared. Its foundation stones and the line where the roof joined the eastern gable of the church can be clearly seen. The sacristy which still remains standing was probably built at the same time as the chancel. The masonry in its walls and roof is inferior to that of the church, suggesting a later date.

The most remarkable feature of the Church is the round tower which has been built into the western gable. Its walls are built with much smaller stones than the rest of the building. Leask believed that the tower was a later addition. However, those who have examined the inside of the tower have confirmed that the round tower forms an integral part of the original building. The tower itself is nearly five meters high and contains three storeys. The top storey under the conical cap has four windows facing the cardinal points. The middle storey has a window facing east, and the lowest storey a still smaller window facing west. Entrance to the tower is from the croft through a door which is only one and a half meters high. The entrance to the croft can be seen as a square hole in the vault.

It is fitting that this church, which is called after St Kevin, has

survived better than the other Glendalough churches because
the memory of Kevin still lives on in this valley after fifteen hundred years.

Many people today will ask, who was he and what did he stand
for? What relevance has Kevin for us today as we stand on the
threshold of the twenty first century? What better place to ask
these questions than in the precincts of this ancient church
which bears his name. Kevin was a seeker who found the power
of God within himself through his hermitage and monastic experience. His memory challenges us, calls us and invites us to
ponder the significance of our faith.

St Kieran's Church

Passing through the gate from St Kevin's Church on the way to the river, on the left hand side stand the remains of St Kieran's Church. It was a nave and chancel church but now only a few meters of the walls remain. The windows and doorway have disappeared apart from a few large stones that formed the lower part of the jambs of the doorway. There are remains of another door through the southern wall of the chancel which probably led to a sacristy that has completely disappeared. The church was probably dedicated to St Kieran by the monks of Glendalough because Kevin and Kieran were not only contemporaries but close personal friends. There is a lovely story told in the Lives of Kevin which describes the closeness of their relationship:

> At one time St Kevin went on a visit to St Kieran who dwelt in Clonmacnoise city on the banks of the River Shannon and towards the western confines of Meath province, opposite the territory of Connaught. But three days before St Kevin arrived the abbot of Clonmacnoise had departed this life. The body was then produced upon a bier within a certain church, until Kevin and others should be present to assist in the internment. Our saint arrived at a late hour in Clonmacnoise monastery and he entered the church where the dead abbot's body lay. He commanded all the brethren to go outside as he wished to be left alone with the sacred relics. Doing as they had been commanded, our saint closed the church doors and remained himself within it, until the following day. But some of the brethren remained watching without the door. While St Kevin prayed, St Kieran's beatified spirit is said to have returned to his body and a holy conversation passed between both saints. Their words were distinctly heard by the brethren outside and Kieran asked our saint that as a sign of lasting friendship both should exchange their garments. This was done. The latter holy person, in like manner was covered

with the garments of our saint. Kieran's body, moreover, seemed full of vital heat and his face appeared ruddy in colour. Then St Kevin declared that the deceased abbot had established a fraternity and union with himself and that this extended to the monks of Clonmacnoise and Glendalough. The body of St Kieran being buried with great honour, St Kevin returned towards his own city.[12]

The fact that St Kevin's Church and St Kieran's Church stand so close to each other today is a sign of the closeness of their relationship as monastic leaders and friends. Standing inside the ruins of St Kieran's Church, we can reflect on how we ourselves experience friendship, and remember those who have been our soul friends.

St Mary's Church

Teampall Mhuire

> The earth is at the same time
> mother,
> she is mother of all that is natural,
> mother of all that is human,
> She is mother of all,
> for contained in her
> are the seeds of all.
> *(Hildegard of Bingen)*

Teampall Mhuire, or St Mary's Church, stands in the outer enclosure of the Monastic City as it exists today, and is therefore often missed by visitors. The church is signposted on the left hand side of the main road which leads to the Upper Lake about two hundred meters past the Glendalough Hotel. There is a difficult climb over the wall by the signpost. The path crosses a field and over another stile into the church grounds (*see map, p 43*).

This church has been known by many different names. In Irish, *Teampall Mhuire* means 'The Church of Mary.' When Beranger came to Glendalough in 1779 it was known locally as The Lady Church, which became Our Lady's Church in the writings of Archdall and Ledwich. Price held that because this church was outside the main monastic enclosure, it was *Teampall na mBan* which means The Women's Church. The presence of a church for women in the Monastic City clearly reflects an inclusivism in early Celtic Christian communities, as for example at Clonmacnoise, Inismurray and Inisglora.[13]

St Mary's Church was probably a separate enclosure specifically for the use of women, but within the greater sanctuary of the Monastic City. Whether this church was a convent chapel or simply a church for women in general can never be known for certain. What matters for pilgrims to Glendalough today is that this is the place where the feminine spirit expressed itself in the past and where it can still be touched and appreciated in a powerful way for those who are prepared to stay here for a while.

St Mary's Church is a nave and chancel church, probably dating to around the late tenth century, built on the foundations of an older church. It was originally nave only. The earliest Irish stone churches were rectangular, without a chancel, therefore not separating the priest from the people. At that time, the whole church would have been regarded as a sacred space. The chancel was added probably a century or so later than the original church. Its stonework is inferior.

The doorway in the western gable is the most impressive and the best preserved of all the old doorways in Glendalough. It is built with seven large blocks of granite in the semi-cyclopean style, joined together by a single border or raised architrave on the outside. On the underside of the lintel, clearly visible if you look up as you enter the door, there is a very unusual saltire cross. It is a diagonal cross opening into circles in the centre and at the ends of the arms. Its purpose may have been to mark the entrance to a sanctuary or place of refuge. The door on the north wall of the church was probably added later. There are two windows, the one on the east chancel wall being the most interesting. It is decorated on the outside with a moulding and a key pattern ending on both sides with the heads of animals no longer recognisable.

The dedication of this church to Mary is significant. Old Irish spirituality recognised her central role in God's plan for salvation. From the beginning of the fifth century, Mary was venerated in the eastern and western churches as *Theotokos* or mother of God. She was intimately involved in all the central mysteries of the Christian faith, which found expression in later reflection and devotion in the Rosary.

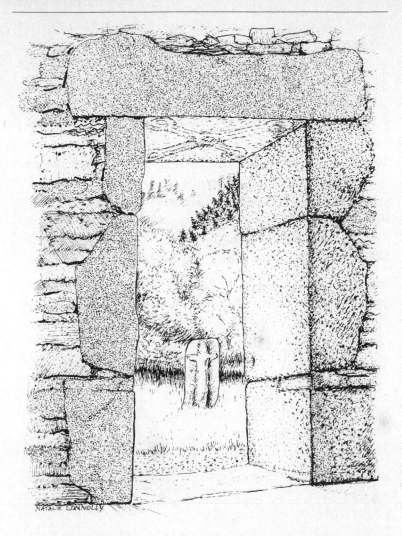

In the north west corner of the church grounds there is a little plot marked by rough boundary stones. Many visitors find themselves drawn to this bleak little place. Here are the graves of infants who died before they received baptism. According to the church's traditional teaching, such children were sent to a place called limbo (or sheol) from which there was no salvation. We can only imagine how the parents of these infants experienced this tradition. In recent times, efforts have been made in various places throughout Ireland to overturn this traditional approach by holding special services of healing and blessing over the graves in question.

In pre-Christian Celtic society, women enjoyed a greater sense of equality with men, for example, in relation to property ownership and inheritance laws. They fought alongside or before men to safeguard and protect the family and community. The Druidic colleges were open to both sexes and, as druids, women held the highest positions of respect and influence in Celtic society. As a result of this tradition of inclusivism, women played an essential part in the development of early Celtic Christianity. This was later neglected due to the growing dominance of patriarchal structures in the church.

In her book, *Celtic Women's Spirituality*, Noragh Jones emphasised the central role of women in the development of Celtic spirituality. She explores how women's spirituality was expressed strongly in many different ways, for example, in the home and family, in loving and mothering, in ritual and religious celebrations, in nature and the seasons, in healing, death and the otherworld.

Feminine archetypes were well established in pre-Christian Celtic society, especially through the worship of the triple goddess and belief in the feminine essence of God which was seen at the heart of creation. With this deeper appreciation for the feminine, women played a central part in all aspects of spiritual formation.[14] It is interesting to note that in the early Celtic churches women also fully exercised ministries as abbots and leaders of monasteries and may have acted as deacons, priests or bishops. There is a very interesting story in the Life of St Brigid, for example, which suggests that the early Celtic churches recognised women's sacramental ministries:

> Brigid and certain virgins went to take the veil from Bishop Mel. He was very happy to see them. Because of her humility, Brigid held back so that she might be the last to whom the

veil should be given. A fiery pillar rose from her head to the roof of the church. Bishop Mel said to her: 'Come, holy Brigid, that a veil may be placed on your head before the other virgins'. Then it happened that, through the grace of the Holy Spirit, the form of ordaining a bishop was read over Brigid. Mac Caille, Bishop Mel's assistant, said that a bishop's rank should not be conferred on a woman. Bishop Mel replied: 'But I do not have any power in this matter. That dignity has been given by God to Brigid, beyond every other woman'. Therefore, the people of Ireland from that time to this give episcopal honour to Brigid's successor.[15]

What contribution did women make to Kevin's Monastic City? Some may have been hermits, others were teachers and soul-friends. One area in which women may have been particularly active in Glendalough is hospitality to refugees and pilgrims. In the Celtic tradition offering hospitality was a sacred ministry. This centred on the mystical belief that any stranger at the door could be a manifestation of the Risen Christ.

In the quietness of the grounds of St Mary's Church, we can pause for a moment to reflect on the feminine influence in our own lives. We acknowledge and give thanks for women's leadership and pray for those who feel called to a particular ministry. We also remember the pain of stillborn hopes, dreams and longings and pray for those who are suffering, that they may find courage and hope for the future.

My soul magnifies the Lord,
and my spirit rejoices in God my Saviour,
for he has looked with favour on the lowliness of his servant.
Surely, from now on all generations will call me blessed;
for the Mighty One has done great things for me,
and holy is his name.

The Green Road

> The footprints of an elder race are here,
> And memories of an old heroic time;
> And shadows of an old mysterious faith,
> So that the place seems haunted
> And strange sounds float in the wind. *(Anon)*

South of the OPW Visitors' Centre, a wooden bridge crosses the river to the Green Road. There is another crossing near St Kevin's Church. The Green Road leads westwards through the woods beside the Lower Lake connecting the Monastic City with the area around the Upper Lake called St Kevin's Desert or St Kevin's Hermitage (Díseart Chaoimhín). The Green Road probably forms part of an ancient pilgrim's way, used by those visiting St Kevin's Bed and Templenaskellig who would have walked this way as they came from coastal areas in the east. Monks travelled this road on their way to and from a time of retreat or solitude in the hermitages by the Upper Lake.

The walk from the Monastic City to the Upper Lake is approximately two kilometers. We invite you to walk in silence, in preparation for your visit to St Kevin's Desert.

Before setting out on the road, why not stand for a while at the place where the two rivers meet? (*See map, p 43*) From here, we can see the Round Tower, St Kevin's Church and the ruins of the Cathedral, all witnessing to the many lives and dreams lived out in this community. Try to form a link with their hopes and dreams in the same way as the waters flow together before you. Perhaps the waters will share their story with us if we take some time to stand and listen. A recent pilgrim returned to this place again and again and drew energy and healing from the movement and merging of the waters. She wrote a poem, which she called 'Conversing Waters'.

You call to me each day
I come to listen to you
Chatting, chuckling, conversing together
Joining hands, mingling fingers over
 tripping stones
Now the throaty, fruity-voiced tones
Now the lighter timbre
Refreshing my tangled brow
Easing out tense furrows deep inside

Together you sooth away my headiness
Together you bring me to my senses
Sometimes in the brightest sunlight
Sometimes through the whipped breeze
Sometimes with the dewy rain
I go my way refreshed
And know that I have prayed.

(Mairead Heaney)

Along the Green Road, near the bridge leading to St Kevin's Church, there is a cluster of granite stones including one with a deep hollow in the centre. This stone is a bullaun which was used in the past for grinding corn and medicinal herbs. The grain or herbs were placed in the hollow of the stone under another stone which fitted perfectly into the hollow. This stone was then turned by means of a stick or handle inserted into it. That is how seeds were ground.

Traditionally this stone is known as the Deer Stone. Sir William Wilde, in his account of the Pattern Day in Glendalough, describes how, on the morning of the Feast Day of St Kevin, 'the Deer Stone was visited by strangers and pilgrims and always found to contain water'. The origin of this name probably goes back to a well known story about St Kevin.

It tells of a chieftain called Colman who divorced his first wife, Cainech, and married again. Cainech became a sorceress and through her magic power, succeeded in killing all Colman's children by his second wife. In the chief's old age, another child

The Deer Stone

was born and after he was baptised and given the name Foelan, his father gave him to Kevin for fosterage. Since Kevin had no milk to feed the baby, he prayed for assistance and immediately a doe came from the neighbouring mountains and provided the necessary food. She continued to come each day until the child grew strong. The milk which she provided was kept in this stone. When the sorceress heard that the child was with Kevin, she went to the mountain called Eanach, overlooking Glendalough, and tried to kill him with her magic spells. Kevin ordered his monks to hide the child and he prayed to God against the power of the sorceress. At this, the sorceress was blinded by the power of God and fell from the mountain down a steep slope into the valley called Cassain, where she died.

There was obviously a passionate and violent conflict fought out between Cainech, her former husband and ultimately with Kevin himself. Was her only interest a jealous revenge on Colman's new family? And why is she said to have become a sorceress? Could this be referring to the wisdom that comes with maturity, or wisdom gained from the old religion, and could it possibly be that it was because of this very wisdom that her husband divorced her? One possible interpretation of this story is that it highlights the violent and destructive struggle between the old religion, which valued women and women's wisdom more inclusively, and the new patriarchal religion of Christianity. The sorceress represents the old ways and the child of the second woman perhaps symbolises the new faith. In this way, Cainech's violence towards these children can be seen as a fight for the very survival of the old religion, and women's place within it.[1]

In contrast to this passionate and terrible battle with all its disharmony and grief, the story of the doe coming to St Kevin illustrates beautifully the co-dependency which is possible between people and animals.

There is a large granite stone in the cluster to the west of the Deer Stone. This is a wishing stone. Traditionally, when making a wish, a person sat in the slight hollow on top of the stone, facing west and leaning backwards until their hands touched the water. In the Irish folk tradition there are many examples of people getting an opportunity to make three wishes, and invariably throwing the chance away. The deepest desire of the human heart is surely a desire to know God. Perhaps many wishes have to be made and wasted before our heart's true desire can at last be acknowledged. What is your deepest wish at this time?

As we stand at the Deer Stone, we gather all these thoughts and questions, and ask for a blessing for the journey ahead. We can use the water in the stone for a blessing in the name of God:

> *Journey Blessing*
> Bless to me, O God
> The earth beneath my feet;
> Bless to me, O God
> The path whereon I go;
> Bless to me, O God
> The thing of my desire;
> Thou evermore of evermore,
> Bless Thou to me my rest.[2]

Walking a short distance along the Green Road, the Lower Lake of Glendalough comes into view. This lake was known in Irish as *Loch na Péist* (The Lake of the large reptile, or monster). According to the legend, Kevin:

> 'banished a great monster from the lesser of the two lakes into the larger one, and as a result sickness of men and of beasts was healed by a visit to the lesser lake. The monster in the other lake takes the illnesses and is thereby left too weak to inflict harm on anybody.'[3]

The story of the monster in the lake is revealing in the light of modern psychology's understanding of the unconscious mind which can have such an impact on our behaviour and responses. It has been said that the history of monsters is the history of humanity's struggle to see its own inner face. Certainly there lurks in all of us 'a little monster' that we tend to push down deep inside us in one way or another. What happens when we consign our dark thoughts into the deep waters of our mind? Do they not tend to re-emerge in 'monstrous' form, perhaps even as the 'monsters' we see in others? What did Kevin do? It appears that he moved the monster to the Upper lake where he himself lived. It might be said that he acknowledged it's presence and tried to befriend it. Perhaps there is a key in that story for each of us.

Water was sacred in Celtic tradition as the feminine source of life and healing energy. Long before Christianity came to Ireland, the Druids used wells and rivers, plants and trees for healing purposes. In his poem, 'Water, My Sister Water', Heldar Camara captures for us something of these sacred beliefs:

Yes, you are beautiful
In the stillness of lakes
In the flowing of rivers
(As humble brooks
Or as the rushing of rapids).
In glittering cascades,
In the oceans which leave in us

> The lingering images of
> The Infinite.

(Helder Camara, *Sister Earth*)

Pilgrims have always come to Glendalough to find healing. There is as much need for this gift today as there ever was. Take an opportunity to wander by the lake or in the forest and reflect on the need for healing in your own life. At the end of this chapter we have included some suggestions for a short healing ceremony which you might try by the shore of the Lower Lake.

Above the road, just beyond the lake, are towering cliffs of mica schist. Find a good place to stop and look at this ancient stone, which is five hundred and twenty million years old. Stratifications within the rock show it was originally formed from layers of eroded sediment at the bottom of the sea. The millions of layers of sediment were eventually hardened by compression and forced upwards by earth movements. Standing beneath the cliffs it is possible to feel a real sense of awe that expresses both insignificance and wonder.

Below the cliffs are many fine old oak trees, including a grove of oaks beside the road on the shores of the Lower Lake. The oak is a symbol of strength and endurance. In pre-Christian religious traditions in Ireland, people worshipped in oak forests and believed that the spirits of the ancestors resided in the oak trees. Long ago, this area had extensive oak forests growing far up the sides of the valley.

The mountain which stands above the oak grove is called Derrybawn (white oak) while the hill on the opposite side is called Camaderry (the bend of the oak). Certain trees and especially oak, hazel, rowan and holly were sacred in Celtic tradition. The Druids are said to have gained knowledge and wisdom from trees. Trees connect heaven and earth and it is possible that those who stay beneath a tree for a while will become deeply conscious of both. The roots connect with our roots and earthy experiences; the branches represent our longing to reach out in search of the light.

We can observe the quality of life which co-exists under the different varieties of sheltering trees. The old deciduous forests of oak, birch and ash provide a haven for the animals, plants and insects. These trees grow in harmony with nature and the elements, allowing sunlight and rain to break through and support life in variety and abundance.

Near the end of the Green Road, on the right hand side in the swampy ground, there is a dense forest of birch trees. The birch is one of the oldest trees in Ireland, with a history going back to the end of the last Ice Age. It is sometimes called 'The Lady of the Forest'. One notices the few old birch trees that stand on their own and the masses of younger birch trees behind them. The older trees have variety and character unlike the others, which are thin and featureless as they struggle to find a little space in the light. The images here are reminders on the one hand of the rugged individualism and strength of the Celtic peoples who lived here in the past and, on the other, of the many people in today's society who struggle to stand with dignity in their own space. There is a beautiful, prayerful atmosphere in this old woodland, which sways gently in the breezes overhead. The forest floor is carpeted with beautiful mosses and other vegetation. Tread softly in this place. You, too, are part of nature's dream. Ask yourself, 'What can I do to take care of the earth?'

Ravens flying over birch woods

A TIME FOR HEALING

My help is in the mountain
Where I take myself to heal
The earthly wounds
That people give to me.
I find a rock with sun on it
And a stream where the water runs gently
And the trees one by one give me company.

(*Nancy Wood*)

Find a suitable place to sit by the lake. Close your eyes and re-member your own journey. Here we can reflect for a moment on the burdens we may have been carrying and our desire for wholeness.

Healing is a gift of God and nature. Take something to represent the demons or difficulties in your own life, perhaps a stick or stone to represent the dis-ease or pain, the guilt or sin or whatever burden, wounds, failures or frustrations you may be carrying. Ask for God's forgiveness and then be prepared to let the waters of the lake take this burden away from you. Throw the object you have chosen into the lake as a symbol of your desire to let go of the burdens you have been carrying.

Notice how quickly the lake becomes calm again after the waters have been disturbed. So it is with God, who can absorb all our un-ease; will always absorb our sorrows, our pains and our penitence. In the way the returning waters cover the surface, so the love of God heals all our wounds and covers us with its protective power.

'Of all wounds, self-inflicted ones go deepest. They are the most difficult to heal, the hardest to forgive, and their scars are impos-sible to conceal.' (Carl Jung)

St Kevin's Desert

Díseart Chaoimhín

O Lonely place,
Floodlit by the sun
You seem to beckon me
Across the lake's dark waters

Why call me?
Why draw my eyes and heart?
You have nothing to offer
Of what the world holds dear

(Eileen Gallagher)

Díseart Chaoimhín or St Kevin's Desert is located at the south-east corner of the Upper Lake. It was probably the original site of Kevin's monastery and has been the hermitage of Glendalough ever since. It has four important stations: Templenaskellig; St Kevin's Bed; St Kevin's Cell and Reefert Church. Before visiting each station, we recommend a visit to the Caher, which is a large circle of stones in the field, near the eastern shore of the lake. The journey can then begin at Reefert Church and proceed to St Kevin's Cell from where a pleasant walk in the woods by Poulanass waterfall can be enjoyed. The best place to view the site of St Kevin's Bed and Templenaskellig is from the Miner's Road on the opposite shore of the lake (*see map overleaf*). The order of visiting each station can be chosen to suit the visitor in the time available.

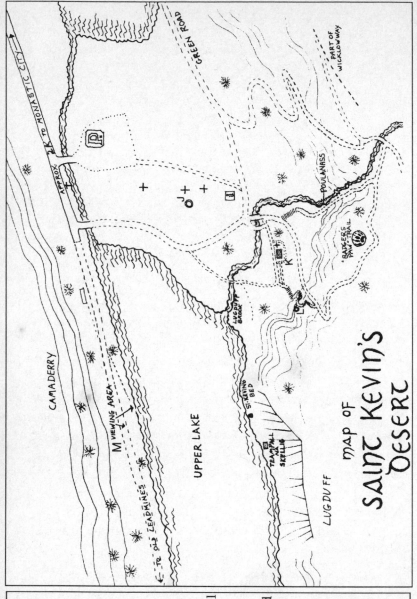

MAP OF SAINT KEVIN'S DESERT

Key

J   The Caher and Pilgrim Mounds

K   Reefert Church

L   Site of foundation stones of St Kevin's Cell

M Place to view St Kevin's Bed and Templenaskellig

The Caher

God bless the world and all that is therein
God bless my house and my children;
God bless the eye that is in my head
And bless, O God, the handling of my hand.
(*Carmina Gadelica* 44)

In the open field at the eastern end of the Upper Lake we find
the remains of an old circular stone fort known as the Caher, the
origins of which remain obscure. It may have been a homestead
in the medieval or early Christian times and possibly dates even
earlier to the pre-Christian Iron Age because of its circular shape
and the unusual thickness of the walls.

The most basic instinct of a human being is that of self-preserva-
tion. In ancient times, every effort was made to protect body and
soul. Banks of earth or walls of stone were built around dwelling
places for security. These walls were topped with wooden poles
or stakes driven into the ground close together. People lived
with danger. There were dense forests all around the country

and wild animals lurked in the shadows. The long, dark nights were particularly frightening. People could not protect themselves in isolation and turned to each other and to God for help.

Many ancient prayers express belief in God as protector. In the Celtic tradition these are called breastplate prayers, similar to enfolding, encompassing and encircling prayers, which all express the need for security. Within ancient homesteads, prayers were being continually offered for protection. Before beginning to pray, people drew a circle around themselves on the ground. It is easy to compose personal encircling prayers using words that best describe the needs of the present moment.

Encircling Prayer

Circle me Lord
Keep protection near
And danger afar.

Circle me Lord,
Keep hope within,
Keep doubt without .

Circle me Lord
Keep light near
And darkness afar.

Circle me Lord
Keep peace within
Keep danger out.

(David Adam, *Tides and Seasons*)

The field around the Caher could be called a Pilgrim's Field. Long ago, when people travelled to Glendalough on pilgrimage, they needed to stay overnight before completing their journey to St Kevin's Bed and Templenaskellig. It is likely that accommodation was provided through makeshift shelters in the field. Beside the Caher there are remains of old stone crosses and small stone mounds known as cairns. The crosses probably marked stations in the days of the Pattern Day pilgrimage. The practice (as in Loch Derg and Croagh Patrick today) was to say prayers around the stone mounds. There is no record of the actual prayers used in the traditional Glendalough stations but it is likely they were said in rounds of seven by the pilgrims as they walked around the cross, seven being regarded as a sacred number by many ancient people including the Celts.

The number seven is linked to many of the old stories of the Celtic saints including, for example, Kevin's seven years as a hermit by the Upper Lake of Glendalough. The practice of walking in prayer around the stones originated in pre-Christian times when people walked in a clockwise direction during religious rituals, following the path of the sun. Christian pilgrims always followed the right hand while remaining faithful to the central movement and practice of the ritual. Why not pray around these old stone mounds and crosses, making up your own prayers and reflections? It would be an appropriate way to remember and continue the ancient traditions of this holy place. A recent pilgrim reflected in this way:

Hallowed stones signs of a people
 Present long ago,
Their dreams founded on things sacred,
Water surging, rushing, finding still
 life within these loughs
A deep peace in this place of God.
I another pilgrim with another dream.
I touch the stones, I stand encircled by them.

Standing within the circle of the Caher it is inevitable that our eyes will be drawn towards the mountains that rise beyond the upper lake. There is a sense of being protected here but also being challenged to discover what is beyond. There is a sense also of being encircled by God. Pause for a moment and imagine yourself being encircled by God's loving care and protection. Is there any special protection you would like to ask for?

Psalm 121
I lift up my eyes to the hills –
from where will my help come?
My help comes from the Lord,
who made heaven and earth.

He will not let your foot be moved;
he who keeps you will not slumber.
He who keeps Israel
will neither slumber nor sleep.

The Lord is your keeper;
the Lord is your shade at your right hand.
The sun shall not strike you by day,
nor the moon by night.

The Lord will keep you from all evil;
he will keep your life.
The Lord will keep your going out and your coming in
from this time on and forever more.

Reefert Church
Burial Place of the Kings

> The spirit animates the body in another
> world. If your deeds are true, death is
> only the centre of a long life.
> *(Lucan the Poet on the teachings of the Druids)*

Reefert Church is one of the earliest Glendalough churches found in the area around the Upper Lake known as *Díseart Chaoimhín* or St Kevin's Desert.

Reefert as we see it today was probably built in the tenth or eleventh century on the site of earlier churches of wood or mud and wattle going back to the time of St Kevin himself. It is a nave and chancel church typical of churches of this period, with an impressive doorway made of granite in the western gable, a simple but beautiful chancel arch of cut granite stones, and a little chancel window opening towards the east. The nave of the church measures approximately nine meters by five meters while the chancel measures four meters by two and a half.

This is a quiet place, mysteriously dark and sombre during the winter when the sun never shines on the southern shore of the lake. In the springtime Reefert Church is like a window through which we see the renewal of life in nature after the cold winter. It is bright and colourful in summer and autumn, when sunlight streams through the canopy of natural woodland. The oak, hazel and birch trees which grow around the church create a natural environment which must be very similar to the forest in Kevin's time.

When this church was reconstructed in the 1870s, it was in a very dilapidated state. The chancel arch and most of the walls, including the southern wall with its two attractive windows, had fallen down. The doorway was standing at that time but it is

Reefert Church, south window, from the inside

likely that it was reconstructed earlier with some of the original stones replaced incorrectly. Like all doorways in churches of this period, the jambs lean slightly towards each other being nearly four centimeters narrower on top than at the bottom.

On the top of the walls at each corner of the building we see projecting corbel stones which supported the external rafters of the roof. This church was probably originally covered with timber or thatch. When Beranger visited Glendalough in 1799 to make sketches of the ruins, he noted that Reefert was called 'The Princes's Church.' Ledwich, who visited the site before Beranger, wrote: 'Reefert Church is literally the Sepulchre of Kings, being the burial place of the O'Tooles, seven of their princes lying there according to tradition'.[1] The land around

Reefert Church, south window, from the outside

Reefert Church has clearly been used as a burial ground during the early Christian period and possibly before. The graveyard holds many ancient crosses and grave slabs which indicate an early foundation. A similar graveyard of the kings can be found on Iona in Scotland.

Reefert is considered to be one of the places traditionally identified with the site of Saint Kevin's tomb. This could explain why later chieftains would wish to be buried here. The earliest evidence for its location comes from the eleventh century when the Life of Kevin was written down for the first time. It is recorded that God sent an angel who urged him to move to a place 'eastwards of the lesser lake' where St Kevin was to have his place of resurrection. When Kevin accepted that he had to move, he called the local chieftain, Dima, and his eight sons, to help him make his transfer. They asked Kevin where the new cells and cemetery were to be located and Kevin answered, 'Here there was formerly a certain shepherd interred and around him many will have their resurrection, for the cemetery will be here.' He then added, 'My sons, cut away the thorns and thistles and make a beautiful spot of this place, for here you yourselves will be interred, for here there will be erected after some time a temple in my name and under its altar you will be interred'.[2]

According to O'Donovan, this is how the name 'The Burial Place of Kings' originated. O'Donovan was convinced that the church built on the site of Kevin's tomb was Reefert, despite the fact that Reefert is not 'east of the lesser lake' but beside the Upper Lake.[3]

In the Celtic tradition the tomb or place of death and burial was always referred to as 'The place of resurrection'. This suggests theological influences from the eastern churches, which emphasised the triumph of life over death in the resurrection of Christ. This is underlined, for example, in the name given to the church in Jerusalem traditionally associated with Jesus' death and resurrection. Since the time of the Crusades it has been known to us in the west as the Church of the Holy Sepulchre, emphasising the tomb, but for the Orthodox Churches present in Jerusalem since before its construction in the fourth century, this church has always been called 'The Church of The Resurrection.' This difference in emphasis is significant and underlines a strong connection between Celtic Christianity and the eastern Orthodox churches from which it took root.

Celtic Christianity emphasised the power of God in creation and the triumph of life over death, which is characteristic of the spirituality of the eastern church. Unlike parts of the British Isles which came strongly under the Roman (Latin) influence, Celtic Christianity absorbed theological influences from the eastern churches, which were incorporated into Celtic religious art, calligraphy and stone carvings, especially the scriptural high crosses. The tradition of eastern iconography, for example, can be contrasted with the crucifixes and statues more commonly found in later western traditions.

Western Church art, perhaps through the influence of Augustinian theology, has tended to emphasise the suffering and sinfulness associated with the ignominy of the Cross, whilst Eastern Christianity emphasised the triumph of life over death, through the resurrection of Christ. Such differences in emphasis have affected our attitudes to Christian spirituality.

Before Christianity came to Ireland, the Druids believed in some form of reincarnation and taught that the soul could manifest itself in various forms, including animals or plants. This belief strongly influenced their attitude to life and death. The Celtic churches shared this strong belief in the immortality of the soul and resurrection of the dead. Eastern theology and pre-Christian Celtic religion combined to give Celtic Christianity a strongly creation-filled, as well as cross-centred, spirituality. We can draw from these traditions in our contemporary concerns for nature and foster a positive Christian spirituality for today.

Standing inside the roofless Reefert Church, it is possible to get a special sense of the power and beauty of the place. Here, the mystery of life and death is one. It is an appropriate place to contemplate the inevitability of our own death and the call to seek the place of our resurrection.

Outside, at the southeastern corner of the church, are seven grave slabs and an old Celtic cross. The cross stands at the centre of the circle, reminding us that our hope for the renewal of creation is the cross of Christ's redemption. Around the cross, within the circle, are ancient symbols carved in stone. The triquestra or Celtic knot is a symbol of eternal union with the eternal God. The interlacing symbols speak of right relationships with God and all creation. A recent pilgrim to Glendalough expressed this desire beautifully in these words:

> Let me not spoil one leaf, nor break one branch,
> Let me not plunder, blunder, pollute, exploit,
> But rather see and hear and touch and taste and smell,
> And in my sensing know you well,
> Creator God.
> *(Marie Connolly)*

In Ireland there is still a strong tradition of remembering the dead. People pray for the dead, believing such prayers are effective. Let us pause a while at Reefert Church and remember our loved ones who have died.

> *Beannacht Dé le hanama na marbh.*
> (The blessing of God on the souls of the dead.)
> *Tá siad imithe ar shlí na fírinne*
> (They are gone on the way of truth.)

The Bresal Stone: 'Pray for Bresal'.
A stone taken from Reefert church

St Kevin's Cell

Go sit in your cell and your cell
will teach you everything.

(From the Egyptian Sayings of the Desert Fathers)

St Kevin's Cell is easily accessible and can be visited after
Reefert Church. From Reefert, cross the stile over the wall which
is found opposite the entrance to the church and follow the short
path through the woods, which leads up some wooden steps.
This leads to the top of a small escarpment on the southern shore
of the Upper Lake. Kevin's Cell can be found on the ledge of
rock overlooking the lake. It is clearly signposted. All that remains today are a few foundation stones, lying in a half-circle
with three oak trees growing up around the stones. The original
cell was a beehive hut built with corbelled, dry stones possibly
with a window overlooking the Upper Lake and a doorway facing the path to Reefert Church.

Kevin's Cell stands between the secluded area of St Kevin's Bed

and Templenaskellig and the monastic settlement of Reefert
Church. The cell was probably visited by pilgrims over the cen-
turies and may have marked an important station on the way to
St Kevin's Bed.

Kevin was a hermit at heart and, like many Celtic saints, his life
was characterised by a deep love of solitude and strict asceticism. Esther de Waal, in her book *A World Made Whole*, explains:

> The anchorites or hermits who were such a distinctive fea-
> ture of the Celtic Church, almost from its earliest days, are an
> example of its marked asceticism. From at least the sixth cent-
> ury anchorites played an important part within the monastic
> movement associated with all the great monastic founda-
> tions. In most cases, the hermit life was regarded as such a
> serious undertaking that it was only to be embarked upon
> after many years in the community and with the approval of
> the abbot. In the 'Rule of the Anchorites' ascribed to St
> Columba, it is made clear that the hermit is to be apart in a
> desert place, in the neighbourhood of a chief monastery.[4]

The cell was at the centre of the hermit experience. It was a place
of solitude and silence but also a place of struggle, where a battle
was waged against temptation and worldly distractions. In this
lifestyle, however, there were dangers in unbridled asceticism,
and it was seen as essential to have spiritual direction and com-
panionship for the soul. In the Celtic tradition this was provided
by the *anamchara* or soulfriend.

Soulfriends shared a deep intimacy and love for each other, with
respect for each other's wisdom. Their relationship was centred
on God. It was honest in its affirmation of the other person but
also very challenging at times. The whole relationship was in-
tended to help individuals make peace with themselves, with
others and with all creation in preparation for death. Ed Sellner
has written extensively about the *anamchara* tradition in his book
Spiritual Mentoring, from which the following quotation is taken:

> For the Christian Celts, influenced by the desert Christians

and their own pagan spiritual mentors, the druids and
druidesses, mentoring and spiritual guidance were considered an important, if not essential, part of spirituality. All the
saints seem to have been changed profoundly by these relationships – whether the soul friends themselves were female
or male, human or angelic, or whether they offered a com-
passionate ear or a challenging word. They were keenly
aware that God is close to those who speak as friends do:
heart to heart. This ministry of the *anamchara*, with its one-to-
one focus, contributed greatly to western culture's increased
emphasis on the integrity and worth of the individual and on
his or her spiritual and psychological development. It also affected the entire history of Christian spirituality, affirming as
it did the conviction that a person's relationship with God
can take the form of effective dialogue and that when sins or
faults, grief or human vulnerability is openly and honestly
acknowledged, healing begins and God's presence is experienced, sometimes unforgettably. As the desert writer John
Cassian suggests, and the stories of the Celtic saints confirm,
soul friendship joins friends together in a common dwelling
that neither time nor space nor death itself can separate: the
dwelling of the soul and of the heart. [5]

It is likely that Kevin exercised this ministry from his cell and
that people came to him to receive advice and spiritual guidance. Perhaps this is how the small communities at Templenaskellig and Reefert Church developed.

Life was hard for the most rigourous ascetics and Kevin certainly
seems to have been one of these. His life must have been a constant struggle. He is said to have dressed only in animal skins
and lived in complete poverty, having renounced all the normal
pleasures of this life. It is a paradox of the hermit life, however,
that while they lived in solitude they were open to friendships
and shared their cell with visitors.

It would be misleading, therefore, to paint a completely bleak
and austere picture of life in the hermitage. Many of the cells

were located in wild, remote, seemingly inhospitable places. But such places were quite often stunningly beautiful especially in fair weather. Even in a location where it would seem impossible to survive, the monks had skills to overcome the onslaughts of the elements and provide for all their basic needs. In some cases the hermitage was, in fact, considered an ideal and rather nice place to be.

St Kevin was never completely alone. His daily life was enriched by a close, harmonious relationship with nature, and he enjoyed unusually close relations with even the wildest animals. There is a well-known story about Kevin and the blackbird which is not found in any of the Lives of St Kevin but was current in Ireland in the twelfth century, and was recorded by Giraldus Cambrensis (Gerald of Wales).

On one occasion during Lent, as was his custom, St Kevin fled from the company of monks and went to a cell in search of greater solitude. He found a small hut which kept out the sun and rain, and spent some time alone, reading and praying in deep contemplation. One day, when he was praying the cross vigil with his arms outstretched through the window of his cell, a blackbird came and made a nest in his hand, in which she layed an egg. Kevin kept silence and continued his prayers, not wanting to disturb the bird and remained completely still until the young bird was hatched.

This is a beautiful story which describes Kevin's closeness to nature, but also draws our attention to the need for stillness. Kevin was practising an exercise well known to many of the early Celtic saints. The cross vigil involved standing or kneeling for considerable periods of time in contemplation, with arms outstretched in the shape of a cross (the sacred tree). As an ascetic, Kevin used ascetic exercises and fasting to deepen his experience of God. He is said to have stood in the cold waters of the Upper Lake for long periods in prayer, especially during the penitential seasons. Seamus Heaney wrote a poem about the blackbird story during his sojourn in County Wicklow:

St Kevin and The Blackbird

And then there was St Kevin and the blackbird.
The saint is kneeling, arms stretched out, inside
His cell, but the cell is narrow, so

One turned-up palm is out the window, stiff
As a cross beam, when a blackbird lands
And lays in it and settles down to rest.

Kevin feels the warm eggs, the small breast, the tucked
Neat head and claws and, finding himself linked
Into the network of eternal life,

Is moved to pity: Now he must hold his hand
Like a branch out in the sun and rain for weeks
Until the young are hatched and fledged and flown.

And since the whole thing's imagined anyhow,
Imagine being Kevin. Which is he?
Self-forgetful or in agony all the time

From the neck on out down through his hurting forearms?
Are his fingers sleeping? Does he still feel his knees?
Or has the shut-eye blank of underearth

Crept up through him? Is there distance in his head?
Alone and mirrored clear in love's deep river,
'To labour and not to seek reward', he prays,

A prayer his body makes entirely
For he has forgotten self, forgotten bird
And on the river bank forgotten the river's name

Seamus Heaney[6]

The sculptor, Imogen Stuart, captures this scene in another way in her woodcarving of St Kevin. It is a picture of an old monk sitting on the ground with bare feet, centred and still and holding the bird in his hand. The bird could represent the restlessness of spirit which it is so necessary to calm and hold still, if the mind and heart are to find a resting place in God. Her carving is so real

it is like a photograph of St Kevin sitting outside his cell and perhaps reflects a more feminine interpretation of the story.

The use of animal symbolism was popular and can be found in
the Book of Kells and other illuminated manuscripts of the same
period. The story of Kevin and the blackbird may therefore have
originated as a veiled teaching on asceticism.

Perhaps we can think of the bird as a symbol for the Holy Spirit.
In St Kevin's Cell, we pray that she will come and make a nest
for the Word in our hearts and that by maintaining stillness, the
significance of the Word and the meaning of the story will become clear to us.

St Kevin's Cell provides an opportunity to rest for a while at this
stage in our pilgrimage journey. It is a holy place, sanctified by
the prayers of numerous saints from St Kevin down to our own
time. It is important to be still here and connect with the Spirit of
God which surrounds this place.

The Cell to enter is no longer a beehive hut made of stones but
the inner cell of the heart. Here we can sit and listen to the
sounds of life all around us slowly moving into a deeper contemplation in silence.

The Hermit's Prayer

Grant me, sweet Christ, the grace to find,
Son of the Living God
A small hut in a lonesome spot
To make it my abode.

A little pool but very clear
To stand beside the place
Where every sin is washed away
By sanctifying grace.

A pleasant woodland all about
To shield it from the wind
And make a home for singing birds
before it and behind.

A southern aspect for the heat,
A stream along its foot
A smooth green lawn with rich topsoil
propitious to all fruit.

My choice of those to live with me
And pray to God as well;
Quiet friends of humble mind
Their number I shall tell.

A lovely church, a home for God,
Bedecked with linen fine,
Where o'er the white Gospel page
The Gospel candles shine.

A little house where all may dwell
And body's care be sought,
Where none shows lust or arrogance,
None thinks an evil thought.

And all I ask for housekeeping
I get and pay no fees,
Leeks from the garden, poultry, game,
Salmon, fruit and bees.

My share of clothing and of food
From the King of fairest face,
And I to sit at times alone
And pray in every place.

(Abbot Manteith, sixth century)

A Walk in the Woods

> The beauty of the trees
> the softness of the air
> the fragrance of the grass
> speaks to me.
> *(Chief Dan George)*

At this stage of the journey, we recommend a short walk in the woods. This will take no more than thirty minutes (*see map, p 84*). From St Kevin's Cell continue up the steps on to the forestry road. Take the uphill road until the river is reached. Turn left and follow the path downwards by the river, past the waterfall to the bridge. It is a short walk of two kilometers but it has some steep steps. The walk is marked as Badger Paw Trail, the reason being that there is a sett of badgers in the vicinity.

Long ago hermit cells were probably clustered in these woods around St Kevin's Cell. It was a place of prayer which invites us to pray again today. There are so many ideal places for quiet reflection, resting under a tree either in the forest or on one of the seats provided along the riverbank, sitting by the river or standing by the waterfall.

In the Celtic understanding of God, the world belongs to God and is sacred because it is created by God. Earth and heaven, nature and grace, light and darkness, the visible and the invisible, belong together. There is a real feeling for nature and confidence in the power of God which cares for all living creatures including the plants and animals. Christianity absorbed this love of nature which was strongly present in Druidic religion. St Brigid, for example, took her name from Brig, the Celtic goddess of nature, and Brigid prayed to Christ as 'The Lord of the Elements'. Here we can reflect on the powerful presence of God in nature. Celtic Christianity can help us rediscover a relationship with God whose presence is found at the heart of creation.

Many people like to stop for a rest at Poulanass waterfall. The water tumbling down is an image of the hectic rush of life today. The pool below the waterfall is a reminder of the need to slow down occasionally and rest for a while. The pool is a place of stillness. There is need for a quiet, still place to survive the noise and constant movement that is part of modern living. Here we can reflect on the restless longings of the heart, and ask ourselves how we experience the still deep pools within us.

When this river first flowed some ten thousand years ago, it found its way through a natural fault or weakness in the old rock. It is consoling to know that God's grace often flows through the faults and weaknesses that are part of everybody's life. In the Easter liturgy of the Church, the sin of Adam is referred to as 'a happy fault' because it opened the way to redemption and resurrection in Christ.

There is a beautiful poem by WB Yeats which reminds us that our journey is mysterious and magical. It is a poem full of beautiful imagery and restless longing. It is called *The Song of Wandering Aengus*:

I went out to the hazel wood
Because a fire was in my head
And cut and peeled a hazel wand,
And hooked a berry to a thread;
And when white moths were on the wing,
And moth-like stars were flickering out,
I dropped the berry in a stream
And caught a little silver trout.

When I had laid it on the floor
I went to blow the fire aflame,
But something rustled on the floor,
And someone called me by my name;
It had become a glimmering girl
With apple blossom in her hair
Who called me by my name and ran
And faded through the brightening air.

Poulanass waterfall

Though I am old with wandering
Through hollow lands and hilly lands,
I will find out where she has gone,
And kiss her lips and take her hands;
And walk among long dappled grass,
And pluck till time and times are done
The silver apples of the moon
The golden apples of the sun.[7]

Templenaskellig
(The Church of the Rock)

Where the air is purer,
the skies are clearer
and God is nearer.
(from the Desert Tradition)

Traditionally, the visit to Templenaskellig and St Kevin's Bed marked the climax of the Glendalough pilgrimage. As mentioned in the introduction to *Díseart Chaoimhín*, we recommend

viewing these two sites from the Miner's Road, on the opposite shore of the Upper Lake. The journey to these places is too dangerous to attempt without an experienced guide (*see map, p 84*).

Templenaskellig is built on a remote spur of land on the southern shore of the Upper Lake. According to Leask, 'The whole site is an example of a monastic settlement, small but complete in itself with the dwelling and burial place of the monks grouped closely with the church they served'.[8]

It is possible that the original church on this site dates back to the time of St Kevin himself. When he came to Glendalough as a young man, it is thought he first lived completely alone near the Upper Lake. Many years later, as an ordained priest, he came back to Glendalough with a group of followers and founded a monastery. According to the Latin 'Life of St Kevin', the original monastic settlement was located on the same site as the Monastic City, near the Visitors' Centre. It was believed that after the monastery was established there, Kevin retreated to a place of solitude near the Upper Lake.

In the Wicklow Letters (442), John O'Donovan holds the view that the place to which Kevin retired was Templenaskellig:

> And thus he lived for seven years alone in different places in the Upper part of the valley between the mountain and the lake, leading the life of a hermit in continual fasting and watching, without a fire, without a house and it is held uncertain whether he supported his life with the roots of herbs or the fruit of trees or with heavenly food, because he himself made it known to nobody. But his monks (afterwards) built a famous cell in the desert where St Coemgen dwelt between the Upper Lake and the mountain on the southern side where there is now a famous monastery in which very pious men always dwell. And that is called in the Scotic *Disert Coemgen* which sounds in Latin *Heremus Coemgen*, that is, the Desert of Coemgen'.[9]

Templenaskellig church is smaller than Reefert or Trinity but with a similar doorway common to all early Irish stone churches. That means the present church was built in the late tenth or eleventh centuries but probably on much older foundations. This church was in a very dilapidated state when it was recon- structed in the 1870s. The eastern gable was rebuilt with its double, round-headed window but the great doorway remains in a collapsed state. It seems a pity that it was not reconstructed especially as the granite stones, including the lintel which was in the original doorway, lie on the ground close by and could be re- stored. Outside the church door, there are several old stone steps leading to a raised platform about a meter above the level of the church site. There is a paved causeway in the centre of this platform. It is likely that the huts of the monastic community were clustered here. These huts could have been built with mud and wattle and roofed with thatch before they were built in stone.

There are grave slabs outside the east gable of the church and a lovely old cross with four incised squares near its base and concentric circles at the centre and the ends of the arms. The arms of the cross are badly eroded.

Beneath the site of the old monastery at Templenaskellig, the lake stretches out and behind it the great cliffs of mica schist climb towards the sky. Occasionally, a hardy goat or sheep browses on the heights and the tranquillity and silence are only broken by the lapping of waves on the shore or the cry of a raven or falcon overhead. The stone steps leading up from the lake shore are a reminder of the days when boats full of pilgrims came across out of curiosity and a desire to pray in the footsteps of St Kevin.

Here, we can appreciate the simplicity of the place where Kevin first lived in solitude by the Upper Lake, later to be joined by a small group of followers who then built up the original monastic settlement at Templenaskellig. The early Celtic Church probably followed the established pattern of Desert Monasteries in Egypt,

Syria and Palestine where small groups of up to twelve monks gathered around an experienced teacher and lived together in a laura or lavra with the individual cells or hermitages connected by a small pathway. They stayed in solitude and practised asceticism with spiritual exercises during the week, 'anchored' to their cells, perhaps also making baskets or other crafts during the day. They would come together with the other hermits for weekly eucharist and a common meal. Kevin was at heart a hermit standing firmly in the orthodox desert spiritual tradition.

This site is reminiscent of earliest desert monastic settlements and would support the view that the first hermits were centred around St Kevin's Bed at Templenaskellig. If this is true, then the development of the Monastic City further down the valley at the confluence of the two rivers may have taken place at a later time after Kevin's death, when Glendalough emerged as a popular centre of pilgrimage and for those seeking to learn his rule and follow his example.

Why is this beautiful place of woodland and water called a desert? To appreciate this we must first understand monastic traditions of the Eastern Orthodox churches where the roots of early Celtic monasticism can be found in the spirituality of the Desert, pioneered in the fourth century by St Antony of Egypt.

The teaching of the Desert Fathers and Mothers found its way to Ireland from Egypt, Syria and Palestine through its advocates in Gaul; it may also have come through maritime traffic between Alexandria and the West or perhaps even directly through journeys of Egyptian monks. There is an interesting record in the Book of Leinster, for example, of seven Egyptian monks visiting Ireland who were buried in Diseart Uilaig, which is modern day County Antrim in the North of Ireland.[10]

The ideals of desert monasticism and strict asceticism appealed to the instincts and imagination of the Irish Celts, whose heroes were well known for their deeds of bravery and physical endurance. There were many others like St Kevin who maintained solitude and practised asceticism:

All of them followed some stony path, sometimes falling by
the wayside, sometimes stumbling, but always advancing towards their transfiguration, their metamorphosis. There was
a rich reward for those who persevered. God was present in
the desert in a more powerful and real form than many knew
him elsewhere. St Jerome spoke of the desert of the hermits
where God is the host.[11]

Looking across the Upper Lake to St Kevin's Bed and Templenaskellig, we sense that we are looking at something remarkably
similar to St Antony's Cave, found near his monastery in the
Eastern Desert of Egypt, or the hermitages in Wadi Natrun,
north of Cairo, where the anchorites first gathered in the fourth
and fifth centuries to be alone with God in the silence of the
Egyptian desert. How have we managed to lose sight of this connection over the centuries? When monasticism first developed
in Ireland, the Christian Church was united and the influence
from eastern Christianity was significant. The final schism between east and west took place only in 1054 CE and this created
the disunity we experience in the church today. During the so-
called Golden Age of Celtic Christianity (450-1050 CE) there was
no such formal division.

The stones of Templenaskellig stand to remind us of this great ecumenical connection between Ireland and the Holy Land. This can
have far-reaching significance both for ecumenism and the rediscovery of our spiritual roots, and can also help us re-connect
with our identity in the orthodox Christian spiritual traditions
of the church. Today, let us ponder awhile on the origins of this
fascinating place which is called St Kevin's Desert, and enjoy the
spirit of wilderness which can still be found here.

St Kevin's Bed

Go to the place of your greatest fear
and there you will find your greatest strength.

St Kevin's Bed lies at the heart of the Glendalough experience. From this hermitage came inspiration which resulted in the great Monastic City in the lower valley. The cave speaks to us of the courage and commitment which inspired the Irish saints to choose isolated and potentially dangerous places to be alone with God in the solitude of the Celtic Desert. St Kevin's Bed has challenged hermits, saints and pilgrims to experience the vulnerability of the inner self, perhaps facing fears which have to be overcome before the transfiguration of the soul can be fulfilled.

There is a great mystery about St Kevin's Bed, situated as it is in such a lonely and inhospitable place. Sean Doggett, a recent pilgrim, helps us to set this haunting place in its historical and spiritual landscape:

> Little is known of the people who inhabited Ireland before the coming of the Celts. They are referred to as the people of the Bronze Age (c. 2000 BC) and we do know from the passage graves and cromlechs they have left us that they must have been a religious people and that the elements of earth, sun and water were of great importance to them. It was important to them what happened to their souls after death. Bodies, at least the bodies of the great ones, were buried with great ceremony in tombs that took time and trouble and much labour to construct ...

> We can picture a Bronze Age king, standing in Glendalough and pointing to a spot on a cliff on the north-facing shore of the Upper Lake, where he wished to be buried. Men would have hacked and chiselled with their bronze tools whilst hanging precariously from the cliff until they had dug out a cave just deep enough and wide enough and high enough to

accommodate the body of their king. We can imagine the funeral procession carrying the body to the site, perhaps from far away, and manoeuvring it into its final resting place in the dark rock, overlooking the Upper Lake. Perhaps they closed the entrance with a large stone slab, like the tomb of Lazarus, or maybe they left it open to the elements. Perhaps it was plundered for whatever treasures had been placed with the body in the tomb.

St Kevin's Bed, from inside the cave

The small cave known as Saint Kevin's Bed looks like a black window in the rock-face on the southern shore of the lake about ten meters above the water. The entrance is one and a half meters high and less than a meter wide. The depth of the cave is only about two meters. Whilst this cave has always been traditionally known as St Kevin's Bed, it is unlikely that Kevin ever lived there. It is most likely the place where he spent time alone with God, keeping prayer vigils through the night and fasting in solitude during the penitential seasons. In the twelfth century, St Laurence O'Toole followed what he believed to be Kevin's example when he came to the cave during Lent for prayer and solitude, first as Abbot of Glendalough and then Archbishop of Dublin.[12]

In the past, the journey to St Kevin's Bed marked the climax of the Glendalough pilgrimage. Pilgrims were taken by boat to Templenaskellig and then along the lake shore to the bottom of the cliff in which the cave is found. They climbed up the rock face by small, rough hewn steps until they came to a wide cleft in the rock known as the Chair. From there they were given a chance to enter the cave one by one. A guide stood above and supported pilgrims as they were lowered down until their feet touched the floor at the entrance to the cave. It was easy at that stage to bend down and move inside. There is just enough space in the cave for one person to sit comfortably or lie down at full length. It is a dangerous place to visit, with a vertical fall outside the cave of ten meters into the deep waters of the lake. No wonder it was referred to as 'the most horrid and holy wilderness'.

Once inside the cave, the pilgrims had achieved their goal. They made their wish and placed the special intention for which they had made the pilgrimage into the hands of God and St Kevin. One of the special benefits traditionally attributed to a visit to St Kevin's Bed was protection for women during pregnancy and a safe delivery in childbirth. Gabriel Beranger, for example, who visited Glendalough in 1779, said that none of his party dared to climb up to the cave although he noted that women did so every day to lie down inside, in the belief that this would protect them from death in childbirth.[13]

Pilgrims believed God would reward their efforts with both
material and spiritual benefits upon completion of a pilgrimage
to this cave. The austerity and hardship which were experienced
points to the traditional value placed on the penitential approach in the Irish Spiritual tradition.

The cave is inaccessible now; the only safe way to approach it is
by boat and no boats are available these days. However, the
lakeshore opposite St Kevin's Bed and Templenaskellig is an
ideal place to sit for an extended time in meditation and reflection, as we seek to enter into the spirit of prayer of the hermits
who once lived there. Here we can reflect on our own fears,
dreams and ambitions. This is a place to observe and to be silent,
and allow ourselves to be drawn closer to God.

Many recent pilgrims have been deeply affected by their visit to
St Kevin's Bed. Richard Hills, who visited Glendalough and St
Kevin's Bed in 1993, wrote this poem about his experiences:

> It is a pilgrimage of many waters.
> From high and far they come,
> compulsive, joyously footsure;
> leaping from rock through giddy space
> to rounded rock, ceaselessly pressing;
> lingering in sombre plunge pools;
> gliding gravely through fern, root and darkness
> skimming rich as fluid amber
> over stones of indefinable colour
> caught in the ring of time.
>
> Gathering in stillness of the lake's depth
> whose surface upholds an image of sky and hills,
> A world awaiting something to be fulfilled.
> Above reflection the rounded cave invites,
> bone-rock bed of the austere saint.
> Access requires a wild path, a cold drench
> to trouble the upheld image, demands a difficult climb.

Achieved is no place of bodily comfort but
where to observe and to be silent
a socket for a motionless eye
to see itself. As mist and mind
admit pervasive light and
through a diffused sun perceive a presence
touched lightly, and still beyond grasping.

An old drawing of the approach to St Kevin's Bed

St Kevin's Well

LOOK! I beg you, don't ever stop looking
because what makes the world so lovely
is that somewhere
it hides a WELL,
a WELL that hasn't been found yet
– and if you don't find it, maybe nobody will …
(Antoin de Saint Exupery, *The Little Prince*)

To find St Kevin's Well, cross the bridge from the Visitors' Centre to the Green Road. Turn left, following the signpost to St Saviour's Priory. After a hundred and fifty meters, on the left-hand side, between the road and the river, there is a small horseshoe-shaped mound with a hollow in the middle and an opening towards the river. A birch tree grows near this opening.

St Kevin's Well, from the river side

It is fairly easy to find in winter and spring but not in summer when the area around the well is covered with bracken. Sir William Wilde, who visited Glendalough frequently in the second half of the nineteenth century, came upon St Kevin's Well, describing it as 'a very beautiful limpid spring renowned for its curative powers'.[1] Today the well and its environs are sadly neglected and the water often dries up completely during the summer.

In pre-Christian times, wells were associated with the presence of a goddess as a source of fertility. This was one of many feminine archetypes in the Celtic tradition. The well marked an opening to the womb of mother earth, the source of life. Wells sometimes gave birth to rivers which took the name of a goddess; for example, the Shannon, Boyne and Erne. The place from which a well sprang from the earth was regarded as a sacred place, and its water a source of healing, rejuvenation and divine energy.

Ancient wells were Christianised and used as places of baptism by early Christians who quickly acknowledged the sacred nature of wells. The names of goddesses were replaced by those of Christian saints. Many were dedicated to St Brigid, midwife and protector of women in labour.

On the Feast Day of the patron saint people gathered at the wells to drink the water and make prayers and offerings. Cures were sought and expected on these occasions. If a fish was seen in the water while a person was drinking from the well, it was regarded as a sign from the guardian saint that a cure was to be obtained or a wish granted. A special tree (usually a whitethorn) grew beside the well and pilgrims often tied a piece of cloth to its branches or inserted a coin into the tree as an offering. After the prayers were said on the Pattern Day, a festival took place with music, dancing and song. A recent visitor to Glendalough spoke about a custom in Co Tyrone where people went to the local well on New Year's Day and took three sips of water, accompanied by this prayer: 'God bless me and keep me from this day until this day next year'.

One of the most beautiful things about a well is its stillness. Its source is from below, where the water enters quietly, never disturbing the calm surface. Wells are like eyes in the earth and when they are clear, they are as a mirror showing a perfect reflection. It is no wonder that in the past wells were associated with healing, especially of the eyes. We can depend on doctors to treat diseases of the eyes today, but who will provide a cure for the inner eye? It is the inner eye we depend on for clarity of vision and discernment, so we might see the real meaning of our lives.

The holy well can be a symbol of the source of life within from which springs hopes and dreams, desires and ambitions. It can also be a place of healing. Wells need to be cleaned from time to time, otherwise they tend to quickly fill up with dead and useless matter. So too, we need to attend to our inner well, which can so easily become concealed by the clutter of our worldly concerns.

As we sit by the well, let us reflect on the significance of our baptism and ask ourselves how a renewal of those promises made at the beginning of our Christian life might help us again on our pilgrim journey. We might also like to offer a prayer for some healing we need. Can we see clearly how God is asking us to live, within ourselves, with others and in the world around us?

Holy places such as Glendalough are like wells of energy from which we can draw nourishment and inspiration. They have grown through the presence and prayers of those who have visited them through the ages. We also contribute to these wells by our own prayers and presence, enriching them further for those who will come after us. Here we can reflect on the gifts we receive and those we leave behind us for the benefit of others.

'The future enters into us a long time before it happens.' (*Rilke*)

St Saviour's Church

St Saviour's Church is known locally as the Abbey or Monastery. It is situated at the eastern end of the valley past St Kevin's Well about twenty minutes walk from the Monastic City. Those with time to visit it will not be disappointed.

The church is located on the bank of the Glendassan River and is now clearly signposted, opposite a white cottage in the woods which can be clearly seen on the right hand side of the road. A path leads down to the left towards the river, through a grove of conifer trees. The church itself is completely surrounded by evergreen conifers. Fr Des Forristal, in his book on St Laurence, *The Man in the Middle*, says that in many ways it is one of the loveliest churches in the valley, though probably the least visited.[1]

St Saviour's is the latest of the older Glendalough churches, probably dating from the twelfth or early thirteenth century. It is associated with Glendalough's second saint, Laurence O'Toole who became Abbot of Glendalough in 1153. Laurence was probably responsible for the erection of this building along with the chancel of the Cathedral and the Priest's House in the old monastery. In the twelfth century, St Saviour's acted as a small priory for the Canons of St Augustine, a reforming religious order who arrived about the time Laurence was Abbot of Glendalough and Archbishop of Dublin.

The church was a complete ruin, overgrown with trees and brambles, before the restoration work carried out by the Board of Works in 1875-1879. It consists of a nave and chancel about twelve meters by six meters and five meters by three and a half meters respectively. There are two doors and two windows in its south wall. There is another door in the northern wall leading to a large room which may have been the Chapter House or refectory for the monks. This room also has two windows, one in the north wall and one in the gable facing east. There is a stairway within this eastern gable which probably led up to a room located over the vaulted ceiling of the chancel. The chancel was probably roofed with stone like St Kevin's Church.

The outstanding features of the building include the triple-order chancel arch and the double-headed eastern chancel window. Both of these were in a very ruined state before the restoration work was completed. In fact, the only parts of the arch that survived were the three orders of pillars on the right hand side near the entrance and the base of the pillars on the opposite side. These are all decorated with a variety of patterns still in a fairly reasonable state of preservation. Since the right hand pillars are the most authentic part of the old building they deserve special attention.

The inside pillar has interesting decorations on its capital. In the centre is the prow of a boat with flying scrolls interlacing with the hair of small human heads that are carved at the angles of the capital. Their hair, in turn, interlaces with an animal figure on the side of the capital facing the nave of the church (*see diagrams*). The capital of the middle pillar was replaced during reconstruction.

Decorations from the capital on the centre pillar at St Saviour's

Three arches can be seen rising from the three orders of pillars. The outer arch is undecorated. The second arch has chevrons pointing towards the nave and the stones or *voussiers* of the third, inner arch are richly decorated on two sides. There is a variety of carvings of many different designs. Unfortunately, they cannot be seen clearly now and many are badly damaged. The span of the arch, which is over two meters wide, is regarded as a fine example of Hiberno-Romanesque architecture.

The chancel was probably roofed with stone over a vaulted ceiling. The east window was completely restored and is richly decorated. Some stones were replaced incorrectly during the restoration. On one stone there is an animal figure biting its tail and on another, two birds holding a human head between their beaks. There are other designs of flowers, leaves and interlaced knots. According to Wilde, the decorations generally have little Christian symbolism and appear to be Greek in origin. The window is spanned by a chevron-decorated arch. There are two large recesses in the east wall beside the window and three others in the south wall of the chancel. These probably contained cupboards, used to store books, sacred vessels and other objects used during liturgical celebrations. One of the recesses in the south wall is of doubtful origin, with part of a millstone inserted into it.

St Saviour's Priory marks the place in Glendalough where the old order ended and the new order began in the late eleventh century. The old monastery was badly in need of reform, with local political influence determining the appointment of abbots, clerical celibacy disregarded and the sacraments of the Church, particularly marriage, neglected. The diverse groups that made up the monastic community lacked central direction and control.

The reform movement began in the Irish Church at the beginning of the twelfth century and Malachy, the Archbishop of Armagh, became a leading reformer. He introduced the Cistercians and Augustinian Canons from the continent with a view to reforming religious life in Ireland. They were highly organised and centralised with their religious communities housed within one group of buildings which only monks and novices were allowed to enter. This marked a significant change from the inclusivism of community in early Celtic Monasticism. St Laurence and St Malachy became great champions of the reform. It was St Laurence who introduced the Augustinian Canons to Glendalough, setting them up in a place apart from the old monastery. He hoped their disciplined way of life would influence everybody in the valley and bring about the necessary changes.

St Saviour's is a suitable place to reflect on needs for change and reform in the church today and openness to new directions in our own lives. We face the reality that our lives are not written in stone and that we are only pilgrims on earth. In time, even the new order that was established in Glendalough had to give way to change and development. The history of the church suggests that major changes occur about every five hundred years. At the present time, we are in the middle of a very significant period of change. We must all believe that we have a part to play in these changes.

St Laurence O'Toole

Lorcán Ó Tuathaill

St Laurence O'Toole was the most famous Abbot of Glendalough after St Kevin himself. While Kevin was the founder of the monastery in the sixth century, it was Laurence who ushered in a new era of Glendalough's history six hundred years later in the twelfth century. This was a century of great change in Ireland. In the church, the old monastic system gave way to the more organised and vibrant religious orders of the continent such as the Cistercians and Augustian Friars. With political changes and the growth of more urban centres, the diocesan system brought the church more directly under the control of bishops and secular or diocesan priests. The twelfth century was to see the last of the Irish High Kings, the end of early Celtic monasticism and the arrival of the Normans, paving the way for English rule in Ireland.

Laurence O'Toole was at the centre of all this change. He was a contemplative monk, deeply concerned about the needs of the poor. He seems to have accepted high office in the church not for personal glory or self-advancement but for the opportunity it brought to serve and lead the people and the church which he loved. In a time of great political intrigue, especially concerning the appointment of clergy to high office, he received a popular mandate for his appointment to be Abbot of Glendalough at the early age of twenty-five and Archbishop of Dublin nine years later in 1162.

Laurence was born near Castledermot in County Kildare in 1128, the son of a local king called Maurice O'Toole, who was subject to the King of Leinster, Dermot Mac Murrough. His

mother was Dervail O'Byrne. As a child he was fostered by
Donagh O'Connor, the King of Offaly. This was a common practice amongst Irish nobility and was a way of strengthening
friendships between them. At the age of ten, Laurence faced his
first major life crisis when he was sent as a hostage to the court
of Dermot Mac Murrough, who had a burning ambition to become High King of Ireland and was prepared to be ruthless in
the methods he used to achieve that ambition. One way to guar-
antee the loyalty of kings who were subject to him was to de-
mand a son as a hostage. If there was any question of disloyalty
the hostage was either maimed or killed.

Laurence was treated very badly and kept prisoner in a remote
place for two years. Perhaps it was this experience of suffering
and isolation which, like St Patrick before him, gave Laurence a
firm grounding in prayer and trust in God alone, and which
may have influenced his later decision to follow the monastic
life. After two years in captivity, it was agreed that he would be
returned to his father in exchange for twelve of Mac Murrough's
men captured by the O'Tooles. Since neither side trusted the
other, the exchange of prisoners took place in Glendalough
under the supervision of the bishop. Maurice O'Toole was so
glad to have his own son returned that he agreed to send one of
his sons to Glendalough to be educated. Laurence volunteered
and decided to join the monastic community as a novice.

He must have impressed everyone with his depth of sanctity
and strength of character because, when the Abbot of
Glendalough died in 1153, Laurence was the unanimous choice
to be his successor even though he was only twenty-five years
old. His appointment was acceptable not only among his fellow
monks but also the local people and their rulers. This was quite
remarkable because for the previous fifty years all the abbots of
Glendalough, with only one exception, were members of the
O'Cahill family.

Laurence had no selfish interest in the power attached to his
position. When the Bishop of Glendalough died in 1157 he was

the popular choice to succeed him but he declined. He was more interested in feeding the people suffering from the effects of famine, and reforming the spiritual life of the monastic community. For this purpose, he brought in the Canons of St Augustine, a new religious order which had emerged on the continent. He was hoping that many monks from the old Celtic system would follow the example of the new orders and reform their lives. He was a person who led by example, joining the new order and accepting their rule.

In 1162, when the Archbishop of Dublin died, Laurence was chosen to succeed him. Mac Murrough had his candidate and so had the Vikings but the Abbot of Glendalough was so well known and respected that both sides accepted him as a compromise candidate. He became the first Irish Archbishop of Dublin. Those who preceded him were all Vikings who looked to the Archbishop of Canterbury as their head. Laurence changed this allegiance by having his consecration performed by an Irish bishop, a decision which would influence the future course of Irish Church history and national politics significantly. Through his influence, Dublin became a part of Ireland for the first time, with a leader who succeeded in uniting its diverse peoples.

Laurence must have been an ecumenical person who could accept change when it was necessary, hold the middle ground in constructive relations with various parties, but also hold on to the best of Irish traditions which he had inherited from his ancestors.

His aims as the Archbishop of Dublin remained the same as when he was Abbot of Glendalough. He continued a programme of church building and reform of the religious life whilst caring always for the needs of the poor. He was responsible for laying the foundations of the Cathedral of the Holy Trinity, later renamed Christ Church, in Dublin. It is likely that the original crypt of the present Christ Church Cathedral dates to this time. He influenced the secular canons of the cathedral chapter to become Augustinian monks and he joined their community himself, making a commitment to the common life of prayer, fasting and poverty. Dozens of poor people received a meal every day from his table and hundreds of children orphaned and abandoned by their parents were taken into his care.

In his busy life, the only times he had for prayer were the quiet hours of the night. When he needed to renew his strength and spirit, he came to Glendalough where he was always welcomed by his nephew Thomas who had succeeded him as abbot in 1162. It is likely that he used to stay at Templenaskellig spending long hours in fasting and prayer which included night vigils in the cave known as St Kevin's Bed.

In 1164 Roderick O'Connor, the King of Connacht, became High King of Ireland. Dermot Mac Murrough deeply resented this but was forced to accept the decision. He fled to England, seeking the help of King Henry II and the Norman aristocracy. Henry accepted his sworn oath of allegiance and gave him a letter to the Norman Lords of Wales recommending him for support. Henry's designs on Ireland were aided by the Papal Bull *Laudabiliter*, issued by the Pope Adrian IV, which authorised him to take measures to strengthen the Christian faith in Ireland and root out abuses.

The first contingent of Normans arrived in Ireland in 1169 and a much larger force under Strongbow arrived a year later. They came to support Mac Murrough but their real ambition was to gain political advantage in Ireland and seize control of the land. In a short time, the towns of Waterford, Wexford and Dublin fell to the Normans, the Irish Kings under Roderick O'Connor retreating in disarray. Henry II came to Ireland for six months in his efforts to control the power of the Norman lords. He also secured the submission of many Irish Kings and so became King of Ireland, bringing to an end the ancient High Kingship. The Irish Kings were forced to surrender their lands but were granted them back if they swore allegiance to the King. Those who refused or betrayed the oath had their lands confiscated. Laurence O'Toole was deeply involved in all this change. He must have had extraordinary gifts as a leader and mediator to survive. 'In the space of ten years, Dublin had changed from a Viking city to an Irish city and then to an Anglo-Norman city. He, the first Irish bishop, was also to be the last for many centuries.[1]

At the Third Lateran Council, held at Rome in 1179, Laurence succeeded in communicating to the Pope the complexities of the Dublin situation and the other side of the story about Ireland. As a result of these discussions, the city was placed under the influence of the Pope himself and Laurence O'Toole was appointed Papal Legate for all Ireland. He called the Council of Clonfert which was attended only by the western bishops who were all Irish. His influence on the papacy and the Irish church displeased Henry II greatly and when Laurence next visited England he was forbidden to return home. After remaining there for some months he decided to go to France. There he became ill and died in November 1180 in the Monastery of the Augustinian Canons of St Victor at Eu in Normandy.

Thanks to the efforts of the monks at Eu, who collected all the information available about his life and recorded all the miracles that occurred through his intercession, Laurence O'Toole was canonised at Rome in 1225. He is one of the few Irish saints officially canonised. His Feast Day is November 14th, given as the anniversary of his death. His tomb, or place of resurrection, at Eu became a centre of pilgrimage and a great basilica, which is still standing, was built in his honour. In Glendalough his memory seems to have faded with the passing of the centuries but St Laurence O'Toole is one of Ireland's most accomplished church leaders and one of Glendalough's most distinguished residents.[2]

Conclusion

As we come to the end of our pilgrim journey in Glendalough we give thanks to God for the roads we have travelled and the blessings we have received on the pilgrimage. The history of the valley and the story of those who have gone before us inspire and help us to make connections within ourselves. Glendalough is an experience for those who stay in it for some time. The place speaks for itself and gives people space to follow their own dreams and journeys.

We are all individuals but also members of a wider community. As we approach the end of the twentieth century we face huge changes in our society and challenges to our established institutions and beliefs. Alongside these challenges is a new desire to seek and value the importance of a spiritual dimension to life's experiences. We now have easy access to the teaching and traditions of many religions and philosophies, offering a wide choice for those seeking a framework for their faith and beliefs. Our churches, too, are being challenged to change and reform. The desire for greater ecumenism, closer co-operation and understanding are growing all the time.

A very exciting part of this process of change and reform involves the rediscovery of treasures of the past. This in turn can create a greater awareness and openness to the future as we re-discover a sense of religious and spiritual identity. This is nowhere more apparent than in the rediscovery of the teachings and treasures of Celtic spirituality, with all its richness of story and tradition.

As we prepare to leave this enchanted valley, having come to the end of our pilgrimage in Glendalough, let us give thanks to

God for the people whose lives have inspired us on this journey:
St Kevin, Cassayr, St Laurence and all the saints of the Celtic
churches who have left us such a memorial of their faith and
compassion as servants of God and fellow pilgrims of another
age.

Notes

FROM HOLLYWOOD TO GLENDALOUGH

1. See Charles Plummer, *Latin Lives of the Irish Saints*, Vol II, Clarendon, Oxford, 1922, pp 127-161. Also: Charles Plummer, *Vitae Sanctorum Hiberniae*, Vol I, Clarendon, Oxford, 1910, pp 234-258.
2. Liam Price, 'Glendalough – St Kevin's Road' in *Essays and Studies presented to Prof. Eoin Mitchell*, John Ryan S.J. (ed), Dublin, 1940, p 261.
3. Price, p 258.
4. Price, p 262.

THE STORY AND LEGENDS OF ST KEVIN

1. See Lennox Barrow, *Glendalough and St Kevin*, Dundalgan Press, Dundalk, 1992, pp 3-4.
2. John O'Hanlon, *Lives of the Irish Saints*, Vol 6, James Duffy and Sons, Dublin, 1891, p 33.
3. John O'Donovan, *Letters containing information relative to the Antiquities of the County of Wicklow, collected during the progress of the Ordnance Survey in 1838*, Vol 1, Dublin, 1838, pp 166-167. (Typed original copies in the National Library, Dublin).
4. O'Hanlon, p 63.
5. O'Hanlon, p 38.
6. John Irvine, *Treasury of Irish Saints*, Brogeen Books, Dolmen Press, Portlaoise, 1964, p 30.
7. O'Hanlon, p 49.
8. O'Hanlon, p 56.
9. O'Hanlon, p 53 ff.

TRINITY CHURCH

1. O'Donovan, p 191.
2. Sir William Wilde, 'Memoir of Gabriel Beranger', in *Journal of the Royal Historical and Archaeological Association of Ireland*, M.H. Gill, Dublin, 1870, p 103.
3. Noel Dermot O'Donoghue, 'St Patrick's Breastplate' in James Mackey (ed), *An Introduction to Celtic Christianity*, T&T Clark, Edinburgh, 1989, p 45.
4. O'Hanlon, p 51.
5. Translation of St Patrick's Breastplate by Noel Dermot O'Donoghue in Mackey, pp 45ff.

THE MONASTIC CITY

1. Derwas Chitty, *The Desert A City*, Mowbrays, Oxford, 1966.
2. G N Wright, *A Guide to the County of Wicklow*, Baldwin, Cradock and Joy, London, 1827, p 118.
3. Pádraig Ó Riain, 'The Book of Glendalough or Rawlinson B502', in *Éigse* 18, 1981, pp 161ff.
4. See Philip Sheldrake, *Living Between Worlds – Place and Journey in Celtic Spirituality*, DLT, London, 1995, p 33ff.
5. Lennox Barrow, *Irish Round Towers*, Irish Heritage Series, Eason, Dublin, 1985, p 1.
6. Peter O'Dwyer, *Towards a History of Irish Spirituality*, Columba Press, Dublin, 1995, pp 49-50.
7. Robin Flower, *The Irish Tradition*, Lilliput Press, Dublin, 1994, p 53. (quoted in O'Dwyer, p 50.)
8. Wilde, p 114.
9. See H.G. Leask, *Glendalough Official Guide*, Stationary Office, Office of Public Works, Dublin, p 20.
10. See Peter Harbison, *Irish High Crosses*, The Boyne Valley Honey Company, Drogheda, 1994, pp 9-14.
11. Esther de Waal, *A World Made Whole – The Rediscovery of the Celtic Tradition*, Fount, London, 1991, p 118.
12. O'Hanlon, p 45.
13. Price, p 267 (footnote).

14. Noragh Jones, *Power of Raven – Wisdom of Serpent*, Floris Books, Edinburgh, 1994.
15. Edward C Sellner, *Wisdom of the Celtic Saints*, Ave Maria Press, Notre Dame, Indiana, 1993, pp 71-72.

THE GREEN ROAD

1. O'Hanlon, pp 57-58.
2. Alexander Carmichael, *Carmina Gadelica*, Floris Books, Edinburgh, 1992, p 244.
3. See Daithí Ó hÓgáin, *Myth, Legend and Romance*, Ryan Publishing, London, 1990, p 74.

ST KEVIN'S DESERT

1. O'Donovan, p 197
2. O'Donovan, p 197
3. O'Donovan, p 197 ff.
4. Esther de Waal, p 41
5. See Edward C Sellner, 'A Common Dwelling: Soul Friendship in Early Celtic Monasticism', *Cistercian Studies Quarterly*, Vol. 29, No 1, 1994, p 21.
6. Seamus Heaney, *The Spirit Level*, Faber, 1996.
7. WB Yeats, *Selected Poetry*, Penguin, 1991.
8. Leask, p 10.
9. O'Donovan, p 170.
10. Charles Plummer, 'Seven Egyptian Monks in Disert Uilag' in *Irish Litanies*, London, 1925, p 65, 118.
11. Kenneth Leech, 'God of the Desert' in *True God – An Exploration in Spiritual Theology*, Sheldon Press, 1985.
12. Des Forristal, *The Man in the Middle*, Veritas, Dublin, 1988.
13. Wilde, p 448.

ST SAVIOUR'S CHURCH

1. Forristal, p 27.

ST LAURENCE O'TOOLE

1. Forristal, p 73.
2. See Alban Butler, *Lives of the Irish Saints*, London, 1938, pp
    175 ff.

Further Reading

Peter O'Dwyer, *Towards a History of Irish Spirituality*, Columba Press, Dublin, 1995.

Mary Condren, *The Serpent and the Goddess – Women, Religion and Power in Celtic Ireland*, Harper, San Francisco, 1989.

Lisa Bitel, *Isle of the Saints*, Cornell U. Press, 1990.

Esther de Waal, *The Celtic Vision – Prayers and Blessings from the Outer Hebrides*, DLT, London, 1988.

John Matthews, *The Celtic Shaman*, Element, Rockport, MA, 1991.

Noel Dermot O'Donoghue, *The Mountain Behind the Mountain, Aspects of the Celtic Tradition*, T&T Clark, Edinburgh, 1993.

Andrew Louth, *The Wilderness of God*, DLT London, 1991.

Thomas Cahill, *How the Irish Saved Civilisation – The Untold Story of Ireland's Heroic Role from the Fall of Rome to the Rise of Medieval Europe*, Bantam/Doubleday, New York, 1995.

Thomas Clancy and Gilbert Markus, *Iona – The Earliest Poetry of a Celtic Monastery*, EUP, Edinburgh, 1995.

Otto Meinardus, *Monks and Monasteries of the Egyptian Deserts*, American University in Cairo Press, Cairo, Egypt, 1989.

Nora Chadwick, *The Celts*, Penguin, London, 1991.

David Adam, *The Eye of the Eagle*, Triangle/SPCK, London, 1990.

David Adam, *The Cry of the Deer*, Triangle/SPCK, London, 1987.

David Adam, *Tides and Seasons*, Triangle/SPCK, London, 1989.

Michael Mitton, *Restoring the Woven Chord – Strands of Celtic Christianity for the Church Today*, DLT, London, 1995.

Caitlin Matthews, *The Elements of the Celtic Tradition*, Element, Dorset, 1989.

Jack Roberts, *The Sheela-na-Gigs of Britain and Ireland – An Illustrated Guide*, Key Books, Cork, 1991.

Liam De Paor, *St Patrick's World – The Christian Culture of Ireland's Apostolic Age*, Four Courts Press, Dublin, 1993.

James Bonwick, *Irish Druids and Old Irish Religion*, Dorset Press, 1986.

Hilary Richardson and John Scarry, *An Introduction to Irish High Crosses*, Mercier Press, Cork, 1990.

Michael Maher (ed), *Irish Spirituality*, Veritas, Dublin, 1989.

Timothy O'Neill, *The Irish Hand*, Dolmen Press, 1984.

Peter Harbison, *Pilgrimage in Ireland – The Monuments and the People*, Barrie and Jenkins, London, 1991.

Patrick Murray (ed), *The Deer's Cry – A Treasury of Irish Religious Verse*, Four Courts Press, Dublin, 1986.

Jacob Streit, *Sun and Cross – From Megalithic Culture to Early Christianity in Ireland*, Floris Books, Edinburgh, 1984.

Edward C Sellner, *Soul Making*, Twenty Third Publications, 1991.

John King, *The Celtic Druid's Year*, Blandford, London, 1994.

James Charles Roy, *The Road Wet, The Wind Close – Celtic Ireland*, Dufour, PA, 1990.